Infrastructure Software Modules for Enterprises

Flexible Software Systems, Module Use-Cases, and Wireframes

Mohamed Farouk

Apress®

Infrastructure Software Modules for Enterprises: Flexible Software Systems, Module Use-Cases, and Wireframes

Mohamed Farouk
Muscat, Oman

ISBN-13 (pbk): 978-1-4842-3020-6   ISBN-13 (electronic): 978-1-4842-3021-3
DOI 10.1007/978-1-4842-3021-3

Library of Congress Control Number: 2017952365

Cover image designed by Freepik

Managing Director: Welmoed Spahr
Editorial Director: Todd Green
Acquisitions Editor: Nikhil Karkal
Development Editor: Priyanka Mehta
Technical Reviewer: Kamlesh Shah
Coordinating Editor: Prachi Mehta
Copy Editor: Corbin Collins
Compositor: SPi Global
Indexer: SPi Global
Artist: SPi Global

Distributed to the book trade worldwide by Springer Science+Business Media New York, 233 Spring Street, 6th Floor, New York, NY 10013. Phone 1-800-SPRINGER, fax (201) 348-4505, e-mail orders-ny@springer-sbm.com, or visit www.springeronline.com. Apress Media, LLC is a California LLC and the sole member (owner) is Springer Science + Business Media Finance Inc (SSBM Finance Inc). SSBM Finance Inc is a **Delaware** corporation.

For information on translations, please e-mail rights@apress.com, or visit http://www.apress.com/rights-permissions.

Apress titles may be purchased in bulk for academic, corporate, or promotional use. eBook versions and licenses are also available for most titles. For more information, reference our Print and eBook Bulk Sales web page at http://www.apress.com/bulk-sales.

Any source code or other supplementary material referenced by the author in this book is available to readers on GitHub via the book's product page, located at www.apress.com/978-1-4842-3020-6. For more detailed information, please visit www.apress.com/source-code.

Printed on acid-free paper

To analysts, those people who fill the transition gap between ideas and working systems.

Contents at a Glance

Contents

About the Author

Mohamed Farouk is a software engineer with 16 years of practical experience in building portals and business applications for governmental organizations in Oman, UAE, and Egypt. During those 16 years he worked in different positions as developer, team leader, project manager, and analyst. He has bachelor's and master's degrees in computer engineering and is as Certified Business Analyst (CBAP) and Project Management Professional (PMP). Visit his LinkedIn profile at www.linkedin.com/in/mohfarouk.

About the Technical Reviewer

Kamlesh Shah has been in IT for more than 34 years. He has experience in designing and developing software solutions for many verticals. For the last several years he has been into enterprise technology, including middleware and BPM and continuous delivery using data center operating system. He is currently providing consulting services as an application integration architect. He also conducts corporate training to help IT teams get absorbed into the latest open source and legacy enterprise projects.

Acknowledgments

Thanks to my colleague Muna AlSalmi for encouraging me to complete this book and helping me to find the lights in the darkness.

Thanks to my daughter Mai for asking me about the progress of the book every day.

Thanks to my father Farouk and my mother Wedad for their continuous support and for wishing me good luck.

Thanks to my friend Ahmed Sayed for always reminding me of my goals even when I forgot them.

Thanks to my friend Ahmed Yahia, who inspires me with his belief in enhancement by applying Agile principles in all aspects.

Thanks to my colleagues in all companies where I've worked (The Moment Group, Integral Solutions, Nortal, InterTech, Sakhr Software, Global Business Network, and Aria Systems).

Thanks to my colleagues in Oman who work in the Ministry of Education, Ministry of Information, Ministry of Commerce and Industry, and Ministry of Fishing and Agriculture.

Thanks to authors of all the books I have read, for helping me to improve.

Many thanks to the whole Apress team, for their help in getting this book available in the market.

Introduction

Most of the software project teams that develop custom software build their systems from scratch. With limited budgets and time, they concentrate on the business functionality and try to minimize or ignore the infrastructure functionality. This book details the functionalities for infrastructure modules to help project teams reduce the time required to analyze these modules. In addition, after a team implements these modules, the modules can be re-used in other projects and enhanced and improved over time. The book also aims to help beginner analysts know more about the infrastructure modules.

The infrastructure modules covered in this book are the Localization module, Lookups module, Documents module, Persons module, Organization Structure module, Authentication module, Authorization module, Communication Rules module, Tasks module, Workflows module, Notifications module, Follow-Up module, Payments module, and Signatures module. Every module will be explained with high-level use-cases, wireframes, and entities.

After reading this book, you will know what infrastructure modules are and how they interact together and with other business modules. You will learn the main functionalities provided by infrastructure modules and become familiar with their design by exploring the use-cases, wireframes, and entities for each of the infrastructure modules.

The typical reader of this book will be any member of a project team that implements custom portals or software systems to manage the internal and external services provided by public or private sector organizations. This book is for system analysts, business analysts, project managers, programmers, and business stakeholders.

CHAPTER 1

■ ■ ■

Introduction to Infrastructure Modules

There are common functionalities among software systems that make them flexible for administration and tracking. These functionalities can be considered as an infrastructure for any software system and can be organized into modules, which we will call *infrastructure modules*. This chapter introduces these infrastructure modules that provide common functionalities to users and to other modules that handle business operations in an enterprise.

After finishing this chapter, you will be able to answer the following questions:

- What are some different types of software modules?

- What are infrastructure modules?

- What are the relations among infrastructure modules?

- What are extension points and plugins?

© Mohamed Farouk 2017
M. Farouk, *Infrastructure Software Modules for Enterprises*,
DOI 10.1007/978-1-4842-3021-3_1

In every software system, there are two types of modules—business modules and infrastructure modules—as shown in Figure 1-1.

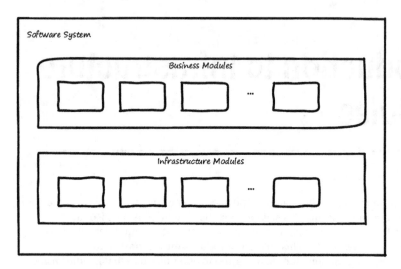

Figure 1-1. *Business and infrastructure modules*

- *Business modules*: These are software modules developed to allow the organization to perform its business (either internal or external). For example, some Enterprise Resource Planning (ERP) modules are considered *internal* business for the organization. Public services provided to citizens, external organizations, or integrated systems are considered *external* business.

- *Infrastructure modules*: These are software modules developed to control how the system will work by providing rules for conducting the business. System admins can manage infrastructure modules to provide flexibility regarding how the software system works and to adapt to required changes in the system.

Infrastructure modules are the core of the system and are independent of the business functionality. They exist as a base on which the business modules are built. This book is devoted to exploring and explaining infrastructure modules.

Types of Infrastructure Modules

Figure 1-2 lists the main infrastructure modules described in this book. These modules are like building blocks for the infrastructure layer. Every module provides a set of functionalities to support the business modules that will be implemented in the system. This section of the chapter briefly introduces each module.

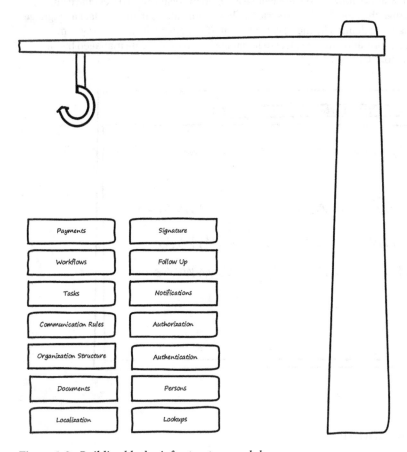

Figure 1-2. *Building blocks: infrastructure modules*

Localization Module

The Localization module manages texts and their translations that will be displayed to the system's users. In countries where English is not the main language, almost every software system will need to be bilingual. In some cases, it may need to be multilingual.

One scenario in which the multilingual software is required is when the organization that owns the software system has foreign employees. These employees need to interact with the system in a language other than the local language. This other language may be English or any suitable language supported by the system. Another scenario is when there is a need to generate reports from the system in foreign languages to be used outside the country. Supporting multiple languages in a software system is known as *localization*.

Figure 1-3 shows how the system will be affected by localization. Users have an option to change the language of the system. This option allows them to select a language from the languages defined by the Localization module. After selection, the system will show the information in the selected language based on the data managed by the Localization module.

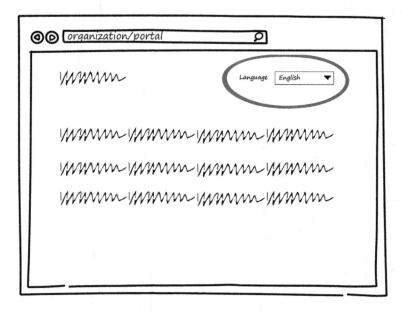

Figure 1-3. *Language selection*

Lookups Module

When filling data form in the system, in some cases the user will need to select some items from a list. This selection can be single selection or multiple selection. Lists that consist of singular items (that is, the item consists of only a name) are called *lookups*. Lookups items can be modifiable or non-modifiable. The Lookups module manages these lists and allows adding, editing, or deleting the items in the list.

Figure 1-4 shows sample of how lookups are used in the system. For example, when selecting a gender, the system displays the values from the gender lookup (male, female), which is defined in the Lookups module. Another example is selection of education level. The system displays a list of values from the education level lookup (bachelor's, master's, PhD, and so on), which is defined in the lookups module. The same applies for communication skills values.

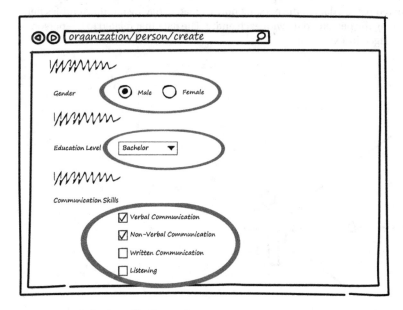

Figure 1-4. *Selection of lookup values*

Persons Module

Every organization's system needs to store and manage persons' data. One *person* in the system may have multiple roles. For example, as you can see in Figure 1-5, a person can be an employee, investor, student, and so on. The system should not repeat the person data. The Persons module manages persons' data and allows adding, editing, or deleting persons. In addition, it prevents the repetition of the persons' data in the system by storing the shared person data in the person entity instead of having multiple entities per role and repeating the person's data with each entity. The data that related to the person's role can be managed by extensions.

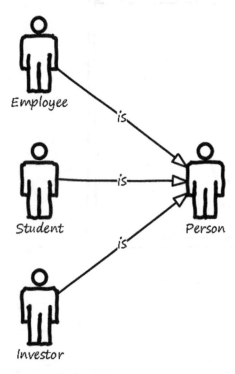

Figure 1-5. *Examples of a person's roles*

Organization Structure Module

Almost any organization consists of departments organized in a hierarchy called the *organization structure*. Every department contains positions filled by employees. Positions also have a hierarchy called a *reporting hierarchy*.

The Organization Structure module manages the departments and their hierarchies as well as the positions and their reporting hierarchies. This module also enables assigning persons to positions to become employees.

Figure 1-6 shows an example of part of an organization structure—in this case, the structure of the General Directorate for Information Technology. Every department has one parent department.

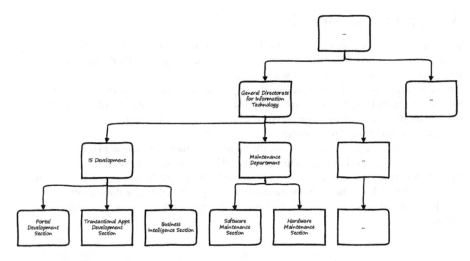

Figure 1-6. *Organization structure*

Figure 1-7 shows an example of a part of reporting hierarchy—in this case, which position reports to which position. One position may report to multiple positions. For example the Programmer position (shown in the figure) reports to both the IS Development Manager and the Maintenance Manager, though one of them will be for primary reporting.

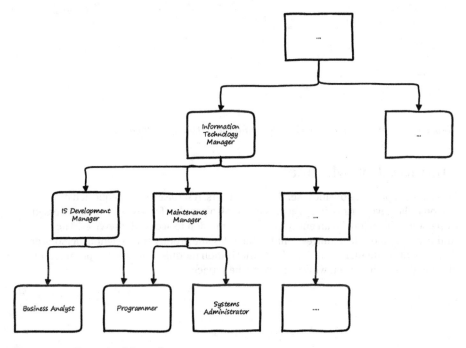

Figure 1-7. *Reporting hierarchy*

Authentication Module

Persons who will use the system need to be *authenticated* by the system in order to recognize them, and before authentication, users need to *register* with the system. Registration can be done via information the person knows (for example, password, username and password, email and password, or mobile number and password) or things the person has (device, ID card, physical token) or via something physical about the person (for example, fingerprint, voice, eye, or face). The registration information can involve a combination of these things.

Based on the registration methods, the system will allow the person to select how to be authenticated and will compare the entered information with the registered information to authenticate the user. The Authentication module manages the registration information and the authentication methods for the persons who use the system.

Figure 1-8 shows a scenario for authenticating a person to perform actions in the system.

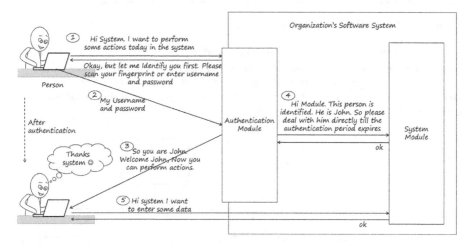

Figure 1-8. *Interaction between a person and the system for authenication*

Authorization Module

Every system provides business services to its users. A *service* can be requested or used by persons who have permission to access it. It is also possible for a service to be accessed by persons who belong to an entity that has permission to access the services. The Authorization module manages defining the roles and groups and assigning persons or departments to them. In addition, the Authorization module manages the permissions given to the entities by allowing or denying the services.

Figure 1-9 shows types of services. Services can be *internal* services for the employees who work in the organization or *public* services provided to clients of the organization.

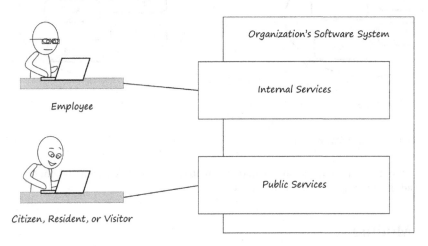

Figure 1-9. *Internal and public services*

The system should know every services it provides along with its description, fees, who is allowed to access it, and so on. This information will be displayed for the users who use the system while they are performing the services.

Persons who use the system are allowed to use some services in the system and perform some functionalities based on their role, group, department, or position. This is called giving *permissions* to the persons or *authorizing* the persons to use a service in the system. Permissions can be given to a person directly, but it is better to give permission to abstract entities like position, group, role, or department. For example, if we give permission to a position, the employee who will be assigned to the position will inherit the permissions for this position, and if the employee is replaced with another one, the old employee will lose the permissions and the new employee will inherit it from the positon.

Communication Rules Module

Some organizations have *communication rules* among positions (employees) or departments. For example, employees are allowed to communicate with their peers, their supervisors, their manager, and their supervised employees. Sometimes there are exceptions in the communication rules. For example, a group of selected employees can communicate with all employees in the organization. Communication rules help in assigning tasks to employees by other employees or in writing correspondence to other employees.

As shown in Figure 1-10, a communication rule consists of *source*, *destination*, and *rule options* to control communications between the source and the destination.

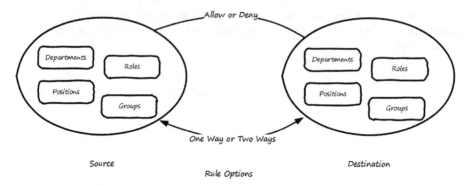

Figure 1-10. *Communication rule*

The Communication Rules module manages who can communicate with whom by allowing adding, editing, or deleting the rules.

Tasks Module

Every person who uses the system may be required to perform a task. The person's task can be created by the person or assigned to them by another person or by the system.

The Tasks module enables the persons to manage their tasks. Persons can use this module to view, create, or complete their tasks. It also allows persons to assign tasks to other persons (delegation) based on the defined communication rules and allow them to monitor the progress of the tasks.

Figure 1-11 shows a scenario for delegating tasks.

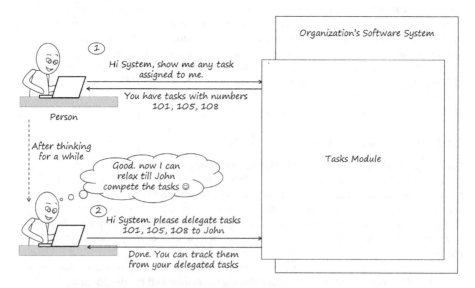

Figure 1-11. *Interaction between a person and the system to delegate tasks*

Workflows Module

All systems require *workflow* to perform a business process. A *business process* is the steps required to provide a service to person or to another organization. Some services provided by the system have an application form that can be filled out manually by persons who use the system or filled automatically by the system or by an integrated system. The application form then goes through steps (*tasks*) assigned to persons who are responsible for performing these steps. After all steps are completed, the service's application is considered completed. It may be rejected or approved. In case of approval, the system modifies its state based on the action associated with the service.

Figure 1-12 shows an example of processing steps for a vacation request. The employee submits the application form, which then goes to the manager for review, at which point the manager can approve or reject it. In case of approval, it goes to an HR employee for review and making a decision. After the decision is made (either approval or rejection), the system will notify the employee. This process is shown from a high level without much detail. However, in the real world a lot of rules and validation will be applied.

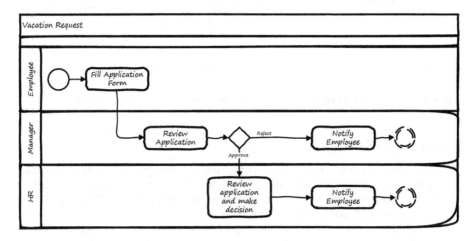

Figure 1-12. *Vacation request workflow*

The Workflow module manages the definition of the service's application, workflow steps and routing, and assigning tasks to responsible persons. It also invokes the required actions to complete the workflow.

Notifications Module

The organization may need to send notification messages to persons who use the system. And persons who use the system may need to receive notifications when changes happened on the system. Notification messages are sent using the preferred notification method for the persons (for example, SMS, mobile, or web notification).

The Notifications module allows users to define their notification preferences and be able to view their notifications. It also allows a system admin to define the default method and enable or disable some methods. And it tracks notifications until they are sent to their destinations.

Figure 1-13 shows a scenario for notification when changes happens in the status of an application submitted in the Workflow module.

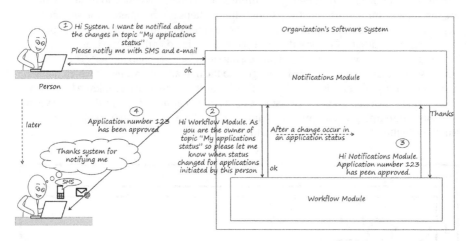

Figure 1-13. *Interaction between a person and the system to receive notifications*

Follow-Up Module

The users of the system may need to follow up an object in the system (workflow instance, task, invoice, payment order, and so on). The Follow-Up module allows the user to select an object and create, modify, or delete the follow-up for this object. The Follow-Up module uses the Notification module to notify the user.

For example, a user may need to follow up a task they assigned to another user. The system will display to the user the follow-up message based on the notification schedule of the follow-up. Figure 1-14 shows a scenario for creating follow-up.

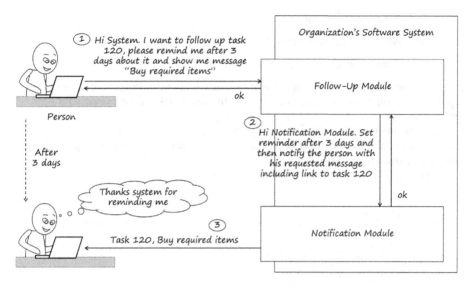

Figure 1-14. *Interaction between a person and the system to create follow-up*

Documents Module

Any software system will require attaching documents based on business functionality. Users of the system should include the attached document information while attaching the document. Document information could be the document type, issue date, notes, and object the document is related to (based on the context where the document is attached—for example, the document may be related to a person, company, invoice, or something else).

The Documents module manages the attached documents by collecting the required information when the users attach documents, providing the ability to search the attached documents, and viewing versions of the attached documents. It also manages the attached documents by providing the ability to search.

Payments Module

As mentioned, organizations provide services, and services can be internal for employees or external for clients. Services often have fees that must be paid. There are many methods to collect payments. For example, payment can be done by any of the following:

- Cash

- Check

- Bank transfer

- POS device

- Online payment gateway

- PayPal or similar services

- Money collection service providers

This means money can be collected online, on the organization premises, or by a partner providing a money collection service. In some cases, paid money can be refunded.

The Payment module allows users to perform the payment operation using the payment methods enabled by the organization, search and view payments registered in the system, and request refunds.

Figure 1-15 shows a scenario of paying by check.

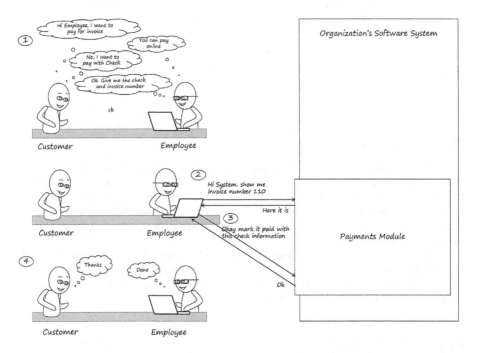

Figure 1-15. Interaction between a employee and the system to pay invoice by check

Signatures Module

The Signatures module manages the operations of validating attached digitally signed documents and generating digitally or electronically signed documents. There are two types of signature: digital and electronic. *Digital* signature involves hashing and encrypting data by the private key of the person or organization who signs the data. *Electronic* signature involves appending the image of the signature of the person who signs the data.

Documents generated by other organization and imported to the system (attached to the system by the users) can be digitally signed. If the system is expecting to receive digitally signed documents, the system will verify those signed documents to ensure their validity.

Documents generated by the system and provided to other organizations (such as reports, certificates, letters, and so forth) can be electronically signed and/or digitally signed.

Using signatures with internal operations inside the organization is not recommended because it adds additional unnecessary effort (though some organizations do ask to include signature in their internal operations).

Infrastructure Modules' Dependency and Extendibility

Dependency exists among infrastructure modules. In other words, some modules need to be implemented first before the other modules can be implemented. In addition, infrastructure modules should be *extendable* to support the business modules that may use them. Plugins can be used to extend the functionality of the infrastructure modules. In this section of the chapter, I discuss dependency and extendibility.

Dependency

Figure 1-16 shows the dependency among infrastructure modules. On the left side of the figure appear three modules that are shared with the other modules. On the right side are the remaining modules that depend on the shared modules.

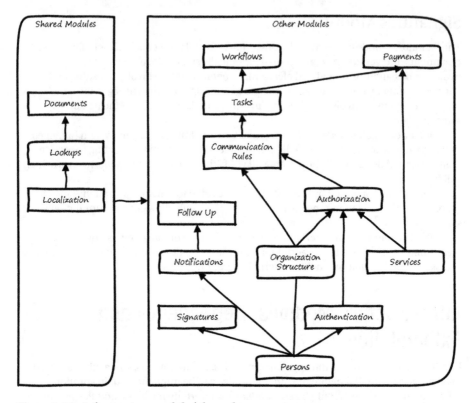

Figure 1-16. *Infrastructure modules' dependency*

The shared modules are Localization, Lookups, and Documents. These modules also have dependency between them. For example, Localization is the first module in the dependency. All modules depend on the Localization module to provide them with suitable text for the language used.

The Lookups module depends on the Localization module. The Documents module depends on the Lookups module because it uses the document types, which are defined in the Lookups module.

All other modules depend on the shared modules. They also have dependency among themselves:

- As shown in Figure 1-16, the Signatures module depends on the Persons module (there should be a person to have a signature). The same applies for Authentication and Notifications. The system cannot authenticate or notify users without having the Persons information.

- The Organization Structure module can exist without the Persons module. However, in order to fulfill the positions in the organization's departments, there is an association between the Persons module and the Organization Structure module.

- The Follow-Up module depends on the Notifications module because Follow-Up notifies users based on the defined follow-up schedule.

- The Authorization module depends on organization structure, services, and authentication because permissions on services are given to positions or departments. In addition, users need to be authenticated before being authorized.

- The Communication Rules module depends on the organization structure and the Authorization module. This module uses the departments, positions, roles, and groups as sources and destinations for the communication rules.

- The Tasks module depends on the Communication Rules module. Communication rules are used when a user wants to assign a task to another user.

- The Workflows module depends on the Tasks module. In order to make progress in the workflow, tasks need to be assigned to the responsible persons and be completed.

- The Payments module depends on the Tasks module. Paying the generated invoices for services requires a task to be assigned to the person who will pay the money or collect the money.

Extendibility

Every infrastructure (or business) module has *extension points* in order to be integrated with other modules, either business modules or infrastructure modules.

The modules that use these extension points implement plugins to be connected to the extension points. Figure 1-17 shows a module that has connection points and plugins.

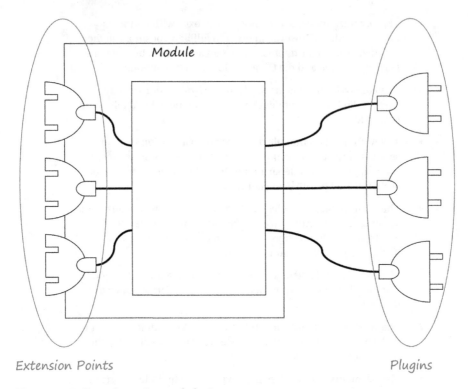

Extension Points   Plugins

Figure 1-17. *Extension points and plugins*

As an example, Figure 1-18 shows that the Authorization module has extension points for the business modules to enable the business modules to provide lists of services and to be included in the Authorization module. This will enable those business services to be configured and will let them be used by the Authorization module, which will manage the authorization of users on these services.

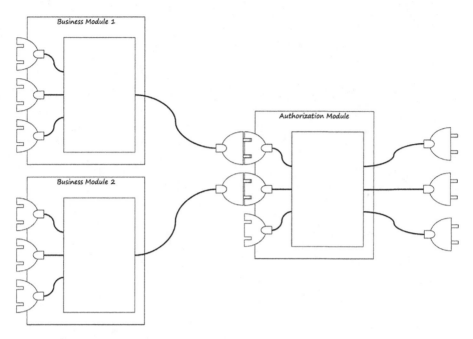

Figure 1-18. *Modules connected together*

Summary

In this chapter, we explored the types of software modules. You learned that there are two types: business modules and infrastructure modules. I gave a brief description of the infrastructure modules and then discussed the dependences among these modules. I provided some examples of dependent modules. You leanred that infrastructure modules have extension points that are used to connect them with other modules.

■ ■ ■

CHAPTER 2

Localization Module

People (persons) who use a software system need to deal with screens in a language understandable to them. They may need to extract reports from the system in a specific language. This means every software system should be flexible in supporting multiple languages and should make it easy for the system's administrators to add new languages or modify system's resources for a specific language. In this chapter, I discuss the Localization module. The Localization module's main functionality is to enable software systems to support multiple languages.

After finishing this chapter, you will be able to answer the following questions:

- Why do you need localization?

- What do you need to localize?

- How and where should you store localized items?

- How should the UI for the Localization module look?

Importance of Localization

People may visit or work in different countries, and each country has its own primary language. Some countries use multiple languages. This means organizations may have foreign employees who speak different languages. The organization interacts with different visitors, residents, or citizens who speak different languages.

Organizations may also need to generate reports in different languages. This means the organization will need to support different languages in the system, and the system should be flexible enough to support multiple languages. With the Localization module, the system administrator can define the languages to be used, the localized images or texts to be shown to users, and localized data to be used.

Items that Are Candidates for Localization

Many items can be localized in a system. The following are examples:

- Labels that appear on system's screens

- Images containing text.

- Images that contain arrows (some languages flow from right to left, others from left to right)

- Audio and video

- Lookup values

- Field descriptions (metadata about a system's entities)

- Entered data (for example, a person's name can be saved in English and Arabic)

- Messages (errors, validation, warnings, and so on)

The Localization module lets the user manage text that appears in the system or is generated by the system. This includes labels, lookup values, messages, errors, and more.

The text to be managed can be stored in the database or in the file system. This module handles both cases and is able to manage the files, which are replicated on multiple servers.

Storing Localizable Resources

In large software projects, the system is installed on multiple web servers. The localized resources may be saved in a centralized place or may be replicated to multiple places. The Localization module can handle both cases. Figure 2-1 shows where resources can be saved.

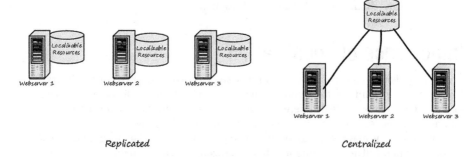

Figure 2-1. *Localizable resources, centralized vs. replicated*

Localizable resources can be saved in a database, in resource files, or in a folder. The Localization module will be responsible for managing the resources by allowing a system admin (or any user who has the privilege) to add languages, provide translation for resources, or modify resources. The remaining of this chapter will discuss the design of the localization module.

Localizable resources' files or table fields must employ a naming convention. There is a base name, which is the main name, and then there is the language part to be appended to it.

For example, if a resource file has a base name Resource1, it can have different names format for a particular language. For example:

- Resource1.en

- Rersource1.English

- Resource1-en

Another example: If a localizable data field in the database has a base name Title, it can have different names for one language:

- enTitle

- EnglishTitle

- Title-en

The Localization module will need to know the naming convention used in order to be able to use the resources for the required language. For example, if a user adds a new language in the system (for example, Arabic), the system will need to add the resource files for this language. For a file named Resource1.en, the new language file will be Resource1.ar.

Localization Module Use-Cases

Figure 2-2 shows some use-cases for the Localization module. Actors for these use-cases are system administrator and system modules. The system administrator is a user who has permission to manage the system. The system module is the software module, which can be a business module or infrastructure module.

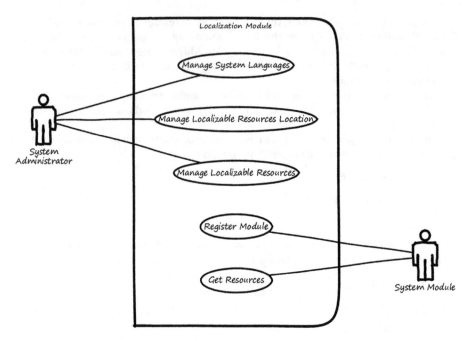

Figure 2-2. *Use-cases for the Localization module*

Here is a description for each use-case:

- *Manage languages*: This use-case is used to add or delete languages that will be supported in the system. It also enables setting the default language.

- *Manage localizable resources location*: This use-case is used to define where localizable resources are located. Localizable resources can be stored in files or in database tables. Depending on the system development strategy, there may be a lot of files and database tables to be used with the modules inside the system. The Localization module needs to know the locations where the resources are saved. This will help by allowing the user to select the resources to be managed and it will help in updating all resources in case of replicated structure.

- *Manage localizable resources*: This use-case is used to modify the resources for each language. It enables the user to enter the resource value (whether that's text, image, audio, or video) for each language used in the system.

- *Register module*: This use-case is used to enable registering a localizable module's information to be included in the system.

- *Get resources*: This use-case is used to provide resource values to other modules when they ask for resources to be displayed.

Localization Module Wireframes

In this section of the chapter, I show you high-level wireframe screens for the Localization module. The UI flow is shown in Figure 2-3.

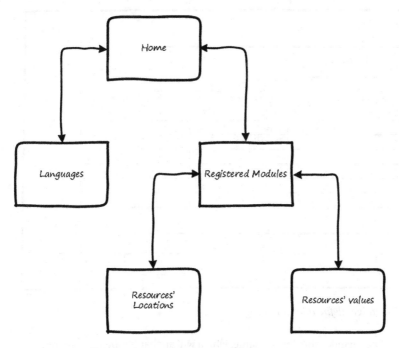

Figure 2-3. *UI flow for the Localization module*

From the home page of the Localization module, the user will be able to navigate to the system's Languages page or the Registered Module page.

Languages Page

This page is used to manage the languages defined in the system. Users can add, edit, and delete languages. Figure 2-4 shows a wireframe for listing defined languages.

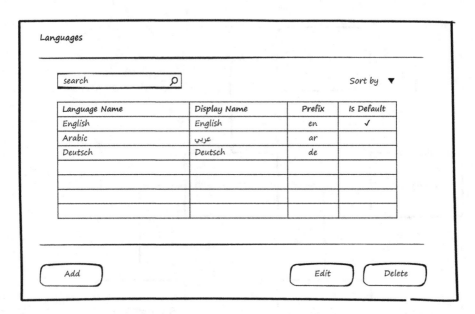

Language Name	Display Name	Prefix	Is Default
English	English	en	✓
Arabic	عربي	ar	
Deutsch	Deutsch	de	

Add　　　　　　　　　　　Edit　　Delete

Figure 2-4. *Languages defined for the system*

Language data includes the display name, which will appear for the users in the UI to select the language. It also includes the prefix, used by the Localization module to recognize the resource files for the currently selected language. One language out of all defined languages may be the default language, which means when users visit the system for the first time they will find the UI displayed in this default language.

Figure 2-5 shows the wireframe for filling in language details.

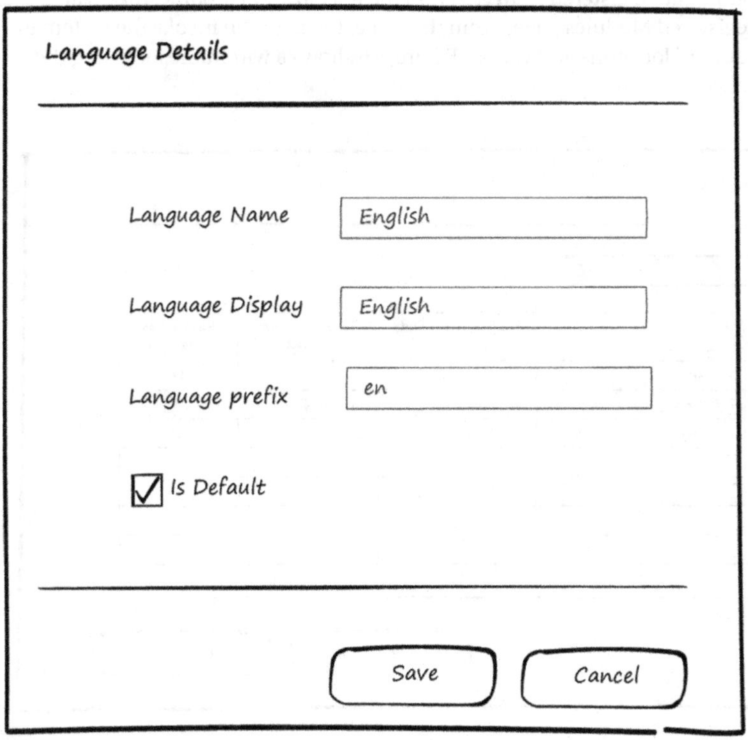

Language Details

Language Name   English

Language Display   English

Language prefix   en

☑ Is Default

Save   Cancel

Figure 2-5.   *Language details*

Registered Modules Page

When other modules are registered (*plugged*) into the Localization module, they will appear in the Registered Modules page. From this page, the user can invoke the system to manage the resources' locations and values. Figure 2-6 shows a wireframe for listing the registered modules.

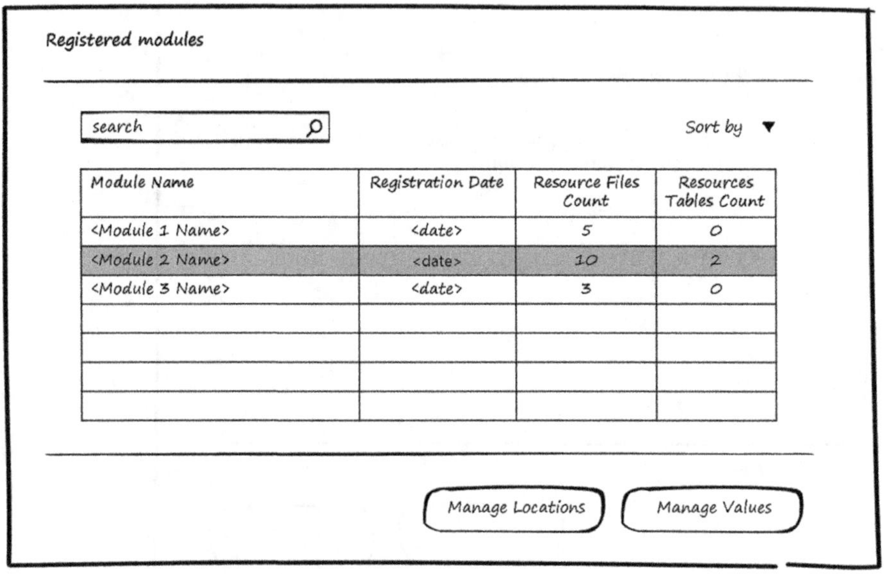

Figure 2-6. *Registered modules to be managed by the Localization module*

Resources' Locations Page

The user can select a module and choose to manage its resources' locations. A module's resources can be either files or database tables. For resources stored in files, every resource file can be stored in one or multiple locations based on deployment structure. The Localization module enables the user to define one location (in the case of a centralized resource file) or multiple locations (in the case of a replicated resource file) for the resource file. The defined locations must be accessible by the Localization module because when resources values in this file change, the module will need to update the values in all locations. Figure 2-7 shows a wireframe for managing resources' file locations.

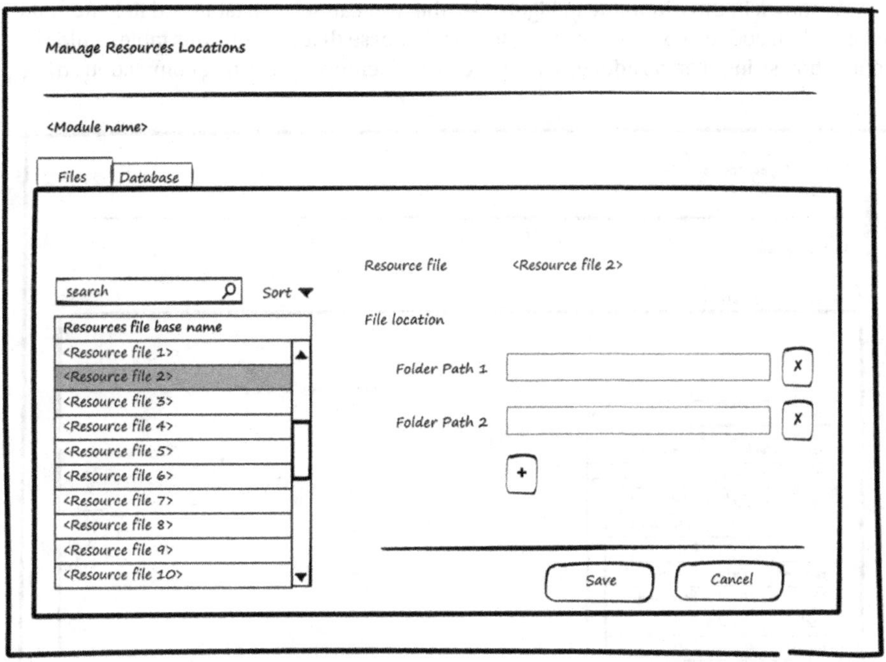

Figure 2-7. *Managing resources' file locations*

The user chooses a file from the list on the left and then can add the folder path that contains this file. Multiple paths can be added. The user can also remove an existing path.

For resources stored in database tables (as mentioned, some fields are localizable), information about their fields is saved when the module is registered. The user can define where those tables are stored (that is, in which databases). It could be in one database, in the case of centralized resources, or in multiple databases, in the case of replicated resources.

As shown in the wireframe in Figure 2-8, the user can select a table and field from the left and then add the connection string for the database that contains this table. Multiple connection strings can be added. The user can also remove an existing connection string.

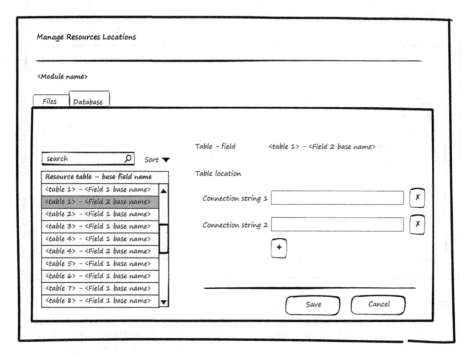

Figure 2-8. Managing resources' database locations

Resources' Values Page

The user can select a module and choose to manage its resources' values. Figure 2-9 shows a wireframe for managing resources' values.

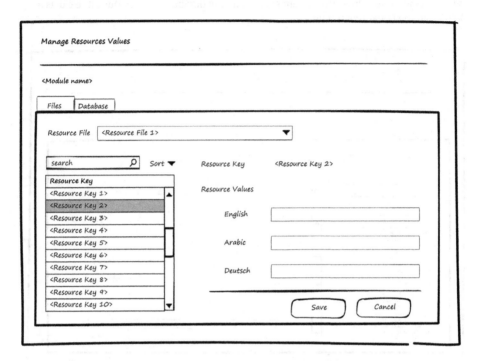

Figure 2-9. *Managing resources' values for resources stored in files*

For resources stored in files, the resource file can be selected from the resource files drop-down list, and the resource keys will appear on the left. When the user selects one resource key, the system enables the user to add or modify the values for this key for all defined languages in the system. When saving these values, the system saves in all the locations defined for this file.

Figure 2-10 shows a wireframe for managing resources' values stored in the database. The table and field can be selected from the resource table's drop-down list, and the resource keys will appear on the left. When the user selects one resource key, the system lets the user add or modify the values for this key for all defined languages in the system. When saving these values, the system saves in all the databases where this table exists as defined in the Locations screen.

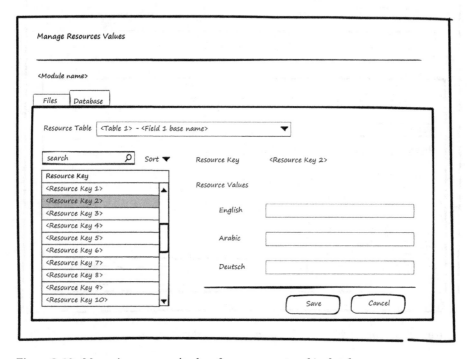

Figure 2-10. *Managing resources' values for resources stored in database*

Localization Module Entities

You've now seen use-cases and wireframes for the Localization module. It's time to have a look at the entities used by the Localization module to store the localization information. Figure 2-11 shows the entities and relations between them.

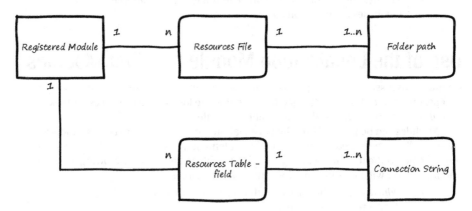

Figure 2-11. *Entities for the Localization module*

Here is a little bit about each entity:

- *Language*: Stores the defined languages in the system.

- *Registered Module*: Stores data about the modules that registered themselves to be managed by the Localization module.

- *Resource File*: Stores data about a resource file—the main data to be stored is the resource file's base name (the name without including the language prefix).

- *Folder Path*: Stores every folder path where the Resource File exists.

- *Resource Table - Field*: Stores data about a resource field in the database. The main data to be stored is the table name and the field's base name (the name without including the language prefix).

- *Connection String*: Stores every connection string for databases where the field exists.

The relations between these entities can be summarized like this:

- Registered Module can have multiple resource files.

- The Resource File can be found in one or multiple folders (folder paths).

- The Registered Module can have multiple Resource Table – Fields.

- The Resource Table – Field can be found in one or multiple databases (Connection Strings).

Use of the Localization Module by Other Modules

Chapter 1 discussed extension points for software modules. The Localization module accepts other modules to be plugged into it so that the localizable resources for these modules can be managed by the Localization module.

Modules can be plugged into the Localization module using the register module use-case. To be registered, modules should implement the register module interface. The interface needs the module to be registered to be able to answer the following questions, and the answer will be used to fill the entities, as described:

- *Who are you?* The answer to this question will be saved in the Registered Module entity.

- *What resource files do you use?* The answer to this question will be saved in the Resources File entity. If information about folders' paths is available, it will be saved in the Folder Path entity.

- *What resource tables do you use?* The answer to this question will be saved in the Resources Table - Field entity. If information about connection strings is available, it will be saved in the Connection String entity.

After a module is plugged into the Localization module, it will be able to use the use-case Get Resources to get a localized value of a resource based on the selected UI language.

Summary

This chapter discussed the localization module, including why localization is required, what needs to be localized, and the naming convention for resource files, which depends on the development method used. I also discussed use-cases for the Localization module and illustrated with wireframes. You learned about the entities and their relations. The last section covered how other modules could use the Localization module.

CHAPTER 3

■ ■ ■

Lookups Module

Users of a software system (persons) need to fill in forms and search for results easily. This means every software system should support the ability to select values for some field from predefined values or previously entered values. These fields are called lookups. What differentiates lookup fields from other fields in the system is that the value of a lookup has a small set of attributes (ID, Name, and Description). The Lookups module's main functionality is to enable software systems to manage lookups and their values.

After finishing this chapter, you will be able to answer the following questions:

- What are lookups?
- Why do you need lookups?
- How and where should you store lookups?
- What does the UI for lookups module look like?

A lookup is a list of ID and name (it also may contain description) for some object. A lookup can be table in the database or it can be enum in the code written by developers.

Importance of Lookups

A lookup contains a list of items consisting of ID, Name, and Description. Lookups are used to make it easier for the user to fill in forms in the system or to search for data. When you use lookups, the user can select from a list of values instead of typing while filling a form in the system.

Lookups are also used because of normalization in the database. Instead of saving the name of the lookup item, the system will save the ID. When retrieving data, the system will look in the lookups and get the corresponding name to be displayed for the ID.

© Mohamed Farouk 2017
M. Farouk, *Infrastructure Software Modules for Enterprises*,
DOI 10.1007/978-1-4842-3021-3_3

Lookups can be sorted into two categories based on the nature of the values of the lookup, called *system lookups* and *user lookups*.

- *System lookups*: These are lookups used by the system. Their items control the behavior of the system because they are used as static parameters in the business rules. We can't add additional items to the lookup until we define programmatically their behavior in the system's code. So, only developers of the system's modules can add items in these lookups.

- *User lookups*: These lookups contain modifiable items that can be modified by the users of the system. Users can add, remove, and edit the items. A user lookup can contain two types of items:

  - *System items*: These are initially inserted in the lookup by developers in the development phase. Those items cannot be removed from the lookup. If additional items are to be added in a lookup as system items, code is written to handle these items in their owning module.

  - *User items*: These items can be added, removed, or edited at any time by the users. If they are used by other entities in the system, the user won't be able to remove them.

The Lookups module enables other modules to register their lookups, and then these lookups will be manageable from the Lookups module. Users who have permission to manage the lookups will be able to add, edit, or remove lookup items based on the way those lookups are registered in the Lookups module.

Lookups Module Use-Cases

Figure 3-1 shows use-cases for the Lookups module. Actors for these use-cases are system administrators and system modules. A system administrator is a user who has permission to manage the system. A system module is the software module, which can be business module or infrastructure module.

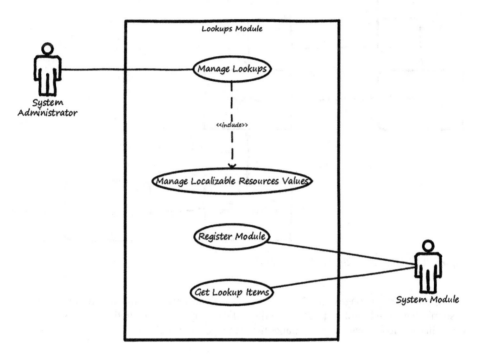

Figure 3-1. *Use-cases for the Lookups module*

Here is a description for each use-case:

- *Manage lookups*: This use-case is used to search, add, modify, and delete items from lookups. It validates the rules of system lookups and user lookups to prevent users from damaging system lookups or system lookups' items.

- *Register module*: This use-case is used to enable other modules that have lookups to register their information. After registration, the lookups for those modules will be manageable from the Lookups module.

- *Get lookup items*: This use-case is used to return lookups items to other modules when they ask for them.

Lookups Module Wireframes

This section shows high-level wireframe screens for the Lookups module. The UI flow is shown in Figure 3-2.

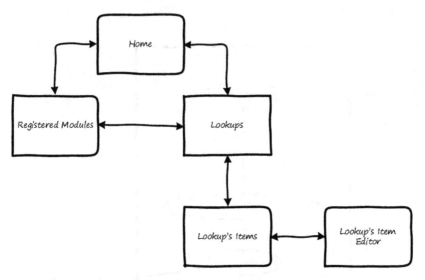

Figure 3-2. *UI flow for the Lookups module*

From the home page of the Lookups module, the user will be able to navigate to the system's Registered Module page. From there the user can navigate to the lookups pages and will be able to navigate to the pages that manage lookup items.

Registered Modules Page

When other modules are registered (*plugged*) into the Lookups module, they will appear in the Registered Modules page. From this page, the user will be able to manage the lookups for each module. Figure 3-3 shows a wireframe for listing the registered modules.

Registered modules for lookups management

search 🔍   Sort by ▼

Module Name	Registration Date	Lookups Count
<Module 1 Name>	<date>	5
<Module 2 Name>	<date>	10
<Module 3 Name>	<date>	3

Manage Lookups

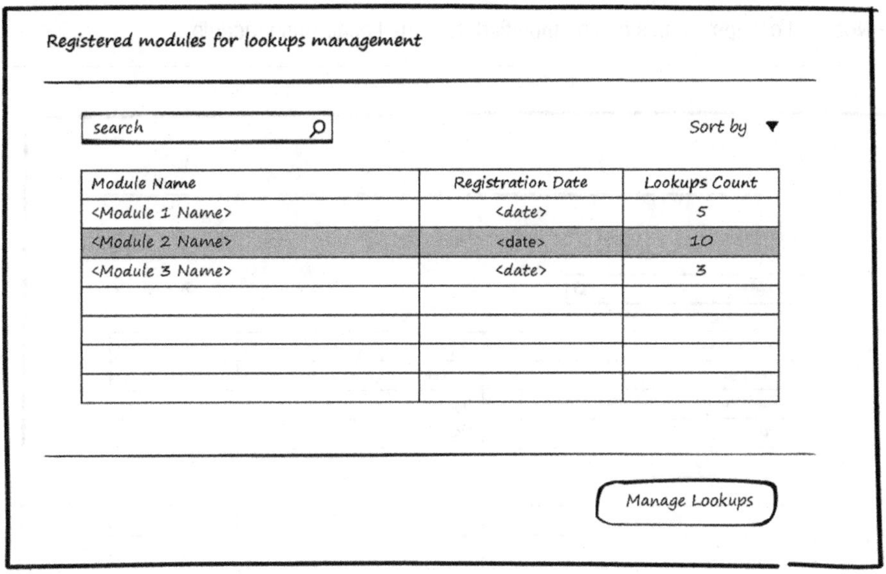

Figure 3-3. *Registered modules to be managed by the Lookups module*

Lookups Page

The user can select a module and choose to manage its lookups. Figure 3-4 shows a wireframe for managing lookups for the selected module. To view the lookup's items, the user will click View Items.

■ **Note**   Lookups' names can be modified from the Localization module.

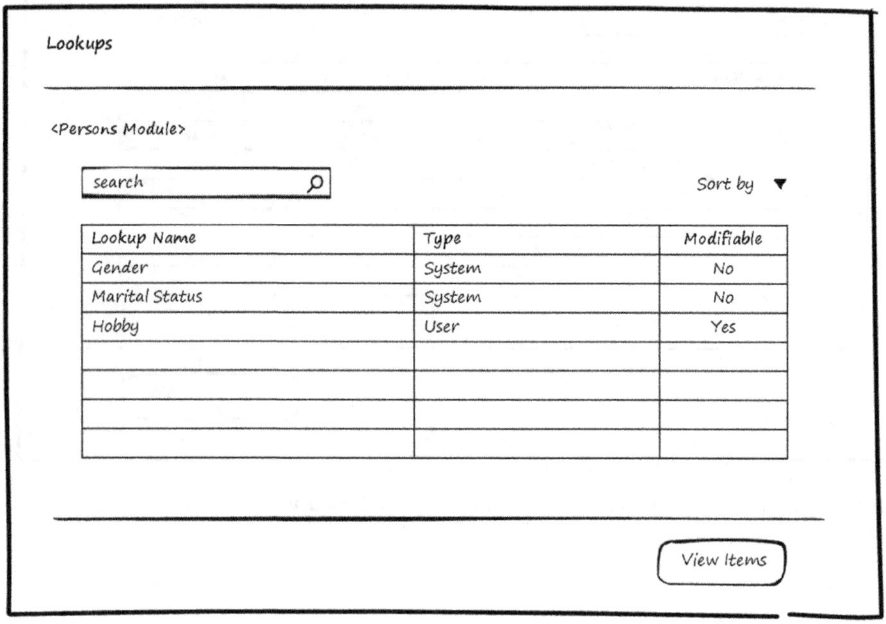

Lookups
_____

<Persons Module>

| search   🔎 | Sort by ▼ |

Lookup Name	Type	Modifiable
Gender	System	No
Marital Status	System	No
Hobby	User	Yes

View Items

Figure 3-4. Manage lookups

Lookup Items Page

Figure 3-5 shows a wireframe for the lookup items. The user can add, edit, or delete lookup items. If the item type is system, the user can't delete it. Every item has a display order, which is used to sort the items when they are retrieved to be displayed in the UI.

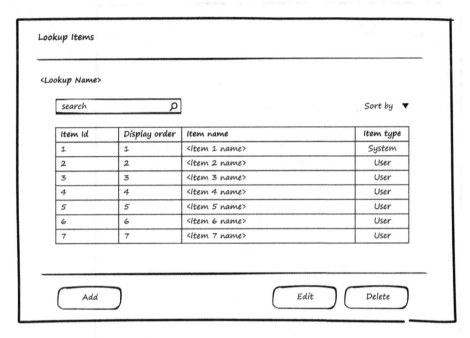

Figure 3-5. *List of items in a lookup*

Lookup Item Editor Page

In Figure 3-6 you see the wireframe for the Lookup's Item Editor page, which can be used for editing or adding new items.

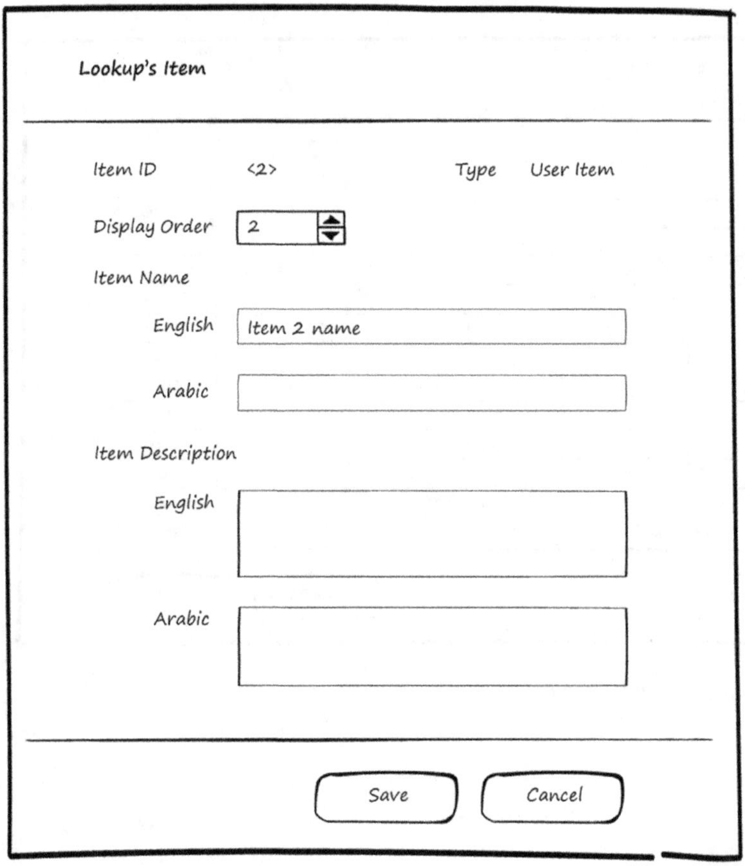

Lookup's Item

Item ID	\<2\>		Type	User Item

Display Order [2 ⇕]

Item Name

English [Item 2 name]

Arabic [ ]

Item Description

English [ ]

Arabic [ ]

[Save] [Cancel]

Figure 3-6. *Edit lookup's items*

This page depends on the Localization module to support entering names and descriptions in the supported languages.

Lookups Module Entities

Now that you've seen use-cases and wireframes for the Lookups module, it's time to see the entities used by the Lookups module to store lookups information. Figure 3-7 shows the entities and the relations between them.

Figure 3-7. Entities for the Lookups module

Here is a description for each entity:

- *Registered Module*: Stores data about the modules that registered themselves to be managed by the Lookups module.

- *Lookup*: Stores data about lookups. The main data to be stored are lookup name, table name (in case lookup items are saved in an entity other than the Lookup Item entity), value field, name field's base name (the name without including the language prefix), type of lookup system or user, and whether it is modifiable or not.

- *Lookup Item*: This is the default entity to store the lookup's items. The registered module can use either this entity or its own tables to store the lookup's items. The main data to be stored are the ID, Name, Description, Type, and Display Order.

The relations between these entities can be summarized like this:

- The Registered Module can have multiple lookups.

- Lookup has multiple lookup items (they can be either in the Lookup Item entity or stored in another entity).

Use of the Lookups Module by Other Modules

The Lookups module accepts other modules to be plugged into it so that the lookups for other modules can be managed by the Lookups module.

Modules can be plugged into the Lookups module using the register module use-case. In order to be registered, they should implement the register module interface and should have the items stored in the format supported by the Lookups module (a lookup item should have a Display Order and an item Type properties). The interface needs the module to be registered to be able to answer the following questions, and the answer will be used to fill the entities, as described:

- *Who are you?* The answer to this question will be saved in the Registered Module entity.

- *What lookups do you use?* The answer to this question will be saved in the Lookup entity.

- *Where are the lookup's items?* The answer to this question will be saved in the Lookup entity.

- *What are the items?* If the lookup items are not stored in specific entities and the module (to be registered) needs to store them in the Lookup Item entity, the answer to this question will be saved in the Lookup Item entity.

After a module is plugged into the Lookups module, it will be able to use the use-case Get Lookup Items to get the items in a certain lookup based on the selected UI language.

Summary

This chapter discussed the Lookups module, including what lookups are, why lookups are required, and use-cases for the Lookups module. I also showed wireframes for the screens and explained the entities and their relations. The last section showed how other modules could use the Lookups module.

CHAPTER 4

■ ■ ■

Documents Module

People (persons) who use a software system often need to attach documents that are required in some forms that they fill in the system. This means every software system should support the ability to define the types of documents and whether they are required or optional. In this chapter, I discuss the Documents module. The Documents module's main functionality is to enable software systems to manage the definition of document types and manage the attached documents and their versions.

After finishing this chapter, you will be able to answer the following questions:

- What are documents, document types, and bundles?

- Why do you need documents?

- How and where should you store documents?

- What does the UI for the Documents module look like?

Documents are files. These files can be of any type, although the system will only allow certain file types to be attached, depending on the business of the organization. Popular file types to be attached to a system include images, PDFs, and in some cases Microsoft Office files (Excel, PowerPoint, Word, and Visio). Electronic documents can be attached directly, but hard copies will need to be scanned and then attached as image files or PDFs.

Document type refers to the business classification for the content in the files. Some examples of document types might include things like ID Card Copy, Medical Report, Passport Copy, Certificate Copy, and so on. This classification enables understating of the content of the attached file. Some document types are common and used in all organizations, and some document types will depend on the business of the organization.

A *bundle* is a collection of documents that are required to be attached in certain scenarios and conditions. A bundle is defined by specifying the document types that will be in the bundle. For example, we can have an Employee Hiring bundle. This bundle will contain the types of documents required from each employee when hired. Types in the Employee Hiring bundle might include Graduation Certificate, ID Card Copy, and Recommendation Letter. Every employee will fill the bundle with their own documents.

© Mohamed Farouk 2017
45
M. Farouk, *Infrastructure Software Modules for Enterprises*,
DOI 10.1007/978-1-4842-3021-3_4

Importance of Documents

Documents are used as evidence. Business services provided by the system will require documents to be attached and be checked by *verifiers* (employees in the organization who receive the requests for services and approve or reject them). The documents could be used to prove something or they can be used to clarify something.

For example, if you are applying for sick leave, you will need to attach a Medical Report document. And if you bought product from a vendor, you will get an invoice. You scan it and attach it to a payment order in the system.

The need for attaching documents while performing a service may be removed if the system is integrated with the other system used in the organization that issued the document. For example, let's say your organization is dealing with one hospital to provide medical checks for the organization's employees, and this hospital has a system that provides web services or web APIs for integration with other systems. Your organization's system is integrated with the hospital system. If you get sick and go to the hospital, your Medical Report will be in the hospital system. When you apply for sick leave, your organization's system will communicate with the hospital system and retrieve the Medical Report data. You don't have to attach documents in this case thanks to the integration that enables systems to communicate and exchange the data.

For cases where no integration exists, though, documents will be attached. These documents need to be organized to be searchable and to not be duplicated. There is no need to attach a document that has been attached before in the system.

The Documents module enables the following functionalities:

- Defining the allowed file types

- Categorizing the files to be attached

- Searching the attached documents for information about them, such as who attached them and from where, and the history of each document

Documents Module Use-Cases

Figure 4-1 shows use-cases for the Documents module. Actors for these use-cases include the system administrator and the system modules. The system administrator is a user who has permission to manage the system, and the system module is a software module, which can be a business module or an infrastructure module.

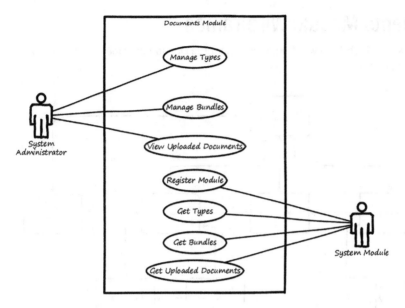

Figure 4-1. *Use-cases for the Documents module*

Here is a description for each use-case:

- *Manage types*: This use-case is used to view, add, modify, and delete document types.

- *Manage bundles*: This use-case is used to view add, modify, and delete definitions of document bundles.

- *View uploaded documents*: This use-case is used to view information about the documents uploaded to the system by users.

- *Register module*: This use-case is used to enable other modules that have document types or bundles to be managed to be able to register their information. After registration, the document types and bundles for these modules will be manageable from the Documents module.

- *Get types*: This use-case is used to return document types to other modules when they ask for them.

- *Get bundles*: This use-case is used to return bundle definitions to other modules when they ask for them.

- *Get uploaded documents*: This use-case is used to return uploaded documents in a bundle to other modules when they ask for them.

47

Documents Module Wireframes

This section shows high-level wireframe screens for the Documents module. The UI flow is shown in Figure 4-2.

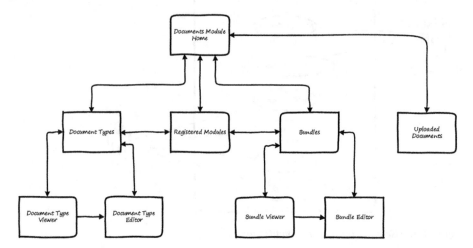

Figure 4-2. *UI flow for the Documents module*

From the home page of the Documents module, the user can navigate to Document Types page where they can manage types, to the Bundles page where they can manage the definition of the bundles, and to the Registered Modules page. From the Registered Modules page, the user can see the types and bundles used by any of the registered modules. If the user wants to see information about the uploaded documents, they can navigate from the home page to the uploaded documents page. In the rest of this section we will see how these pages look.

Registered Modules Page

When other modules are registered (plugged) into the Documents module, they will appear in the Registered Modules page. From this page, the user can manage the document types and the bundles of document types used by these modules. Figure 4-3 illustrates listing the registered modules.

Registered modules for documents management

search 🔍			Sort by ▼
Module Name	Registration Date	Document Types Count	Bundles Count
<Module 1 Name>	<date>	5	2
<Module 2 Name>	<date>	10	1
<Module 3 Name>	<date>	3	3

[Manage Types]　[Manage Bundles]

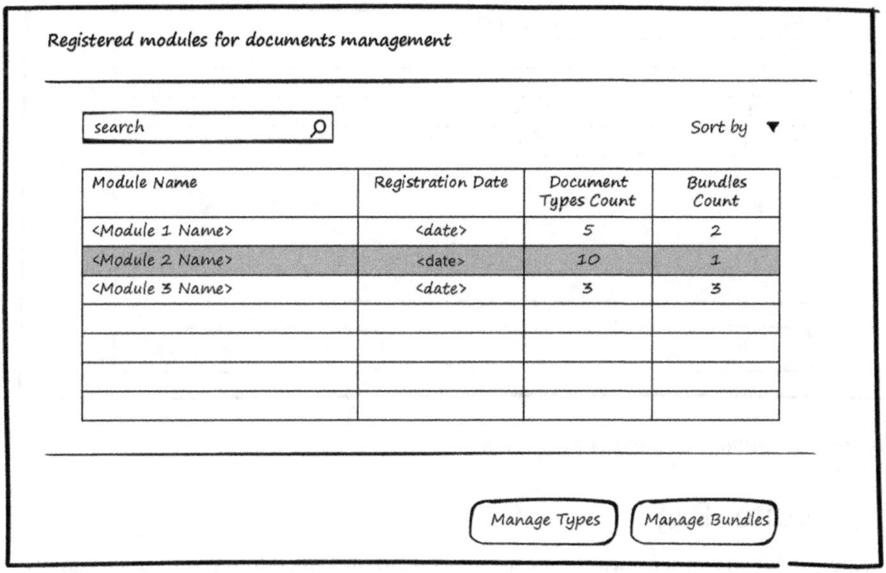

Figure 4-3. *Registered modules to be managed by Documents module*

Document Types Page

This page is used to manage the document types. The user can view, add, edit, and delete document types used in the system. Figure 4-4 shows a wireframe for listing defined document types.

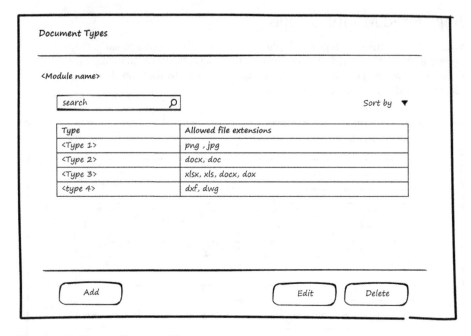

Figure 4-4. *Manage Document Types page*

Type Editor Page

In Figure 4-5, you can see a wireframe for the Document Type Editor page, which can be used for editing or adding document type.

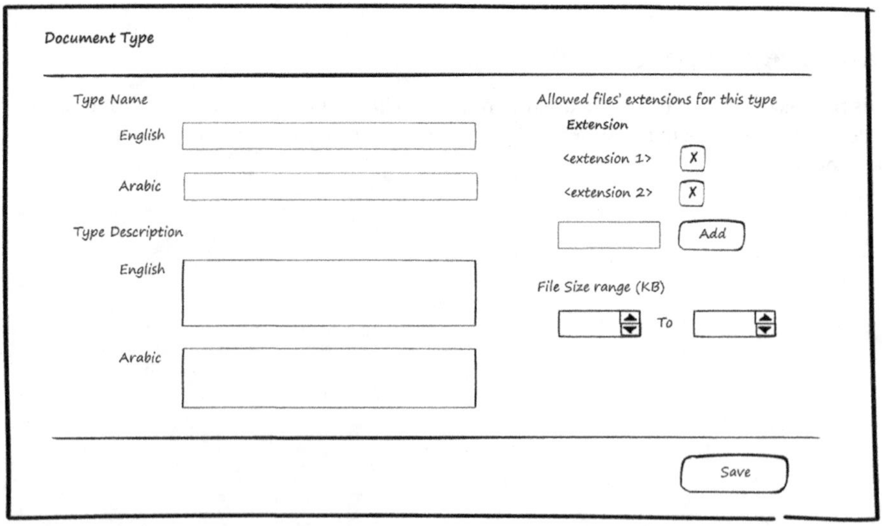

Figure 4-5. *Edit Document Type*

This page will depend on the Localization module to support entering the name and description of document type in the supported languages.

Bundles Page

This page is used to manage the bundles of document types. Users can view, add, edit, and delete bundles used in the system. Figure 4-6 shows a wireframe for listing defined bundles.

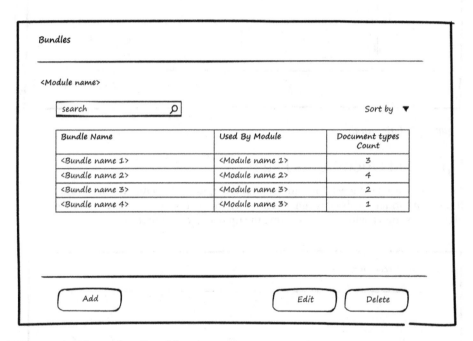

Figure 4-6. *Manage bundles of document types*

Bundle Editor Page

In Figure 4-7, you can see the wireframe for the Bundle Editor page, which can be used for editing or adding bundles of document types.

This page will depend on the Localization module to support entering the name and description of bundles in the supported languages.

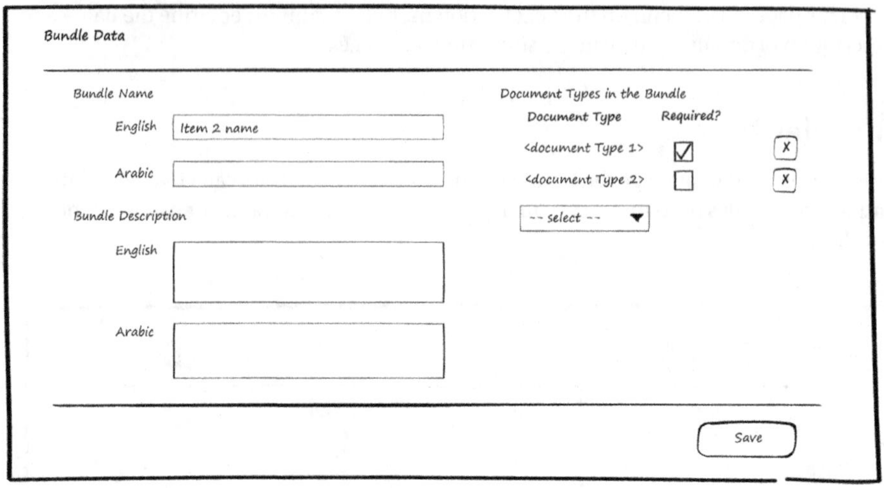

Figure 4-7. *Edit Bundle*

Uploaded Documents Page

This page is used to view information about the uploaded documents in the system. It shows information about when and from where the documents were uploaded. Figure 4-8 shows a wireframe for listing the uploaded documents.

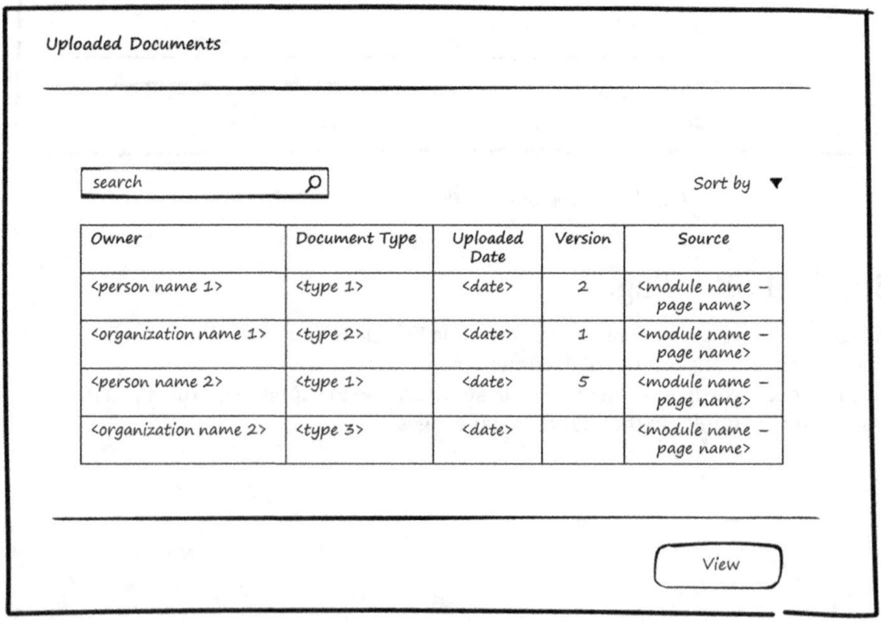

Figure 4-8. *List of uploaded documents*

Uploaded Document Info Page

The user can view more information about the uploaded document by selecting a document and clicking the View button. Figure 4-9 shows a wireframe for displaying uploaded document information.

Document Info

| Document ID | <2> | | Type | Document Type |

Document Owner   <Owner name>

Uploaded By   <Person name or System name>

Available Versions

Version	Uploaded Date	Source	Bundle
3	<date>	<module name – page name>	<bundle name>
2	<date>	<module name – page name>	<bundle name>
1	<date>	<module name – page name>	<bundle name>

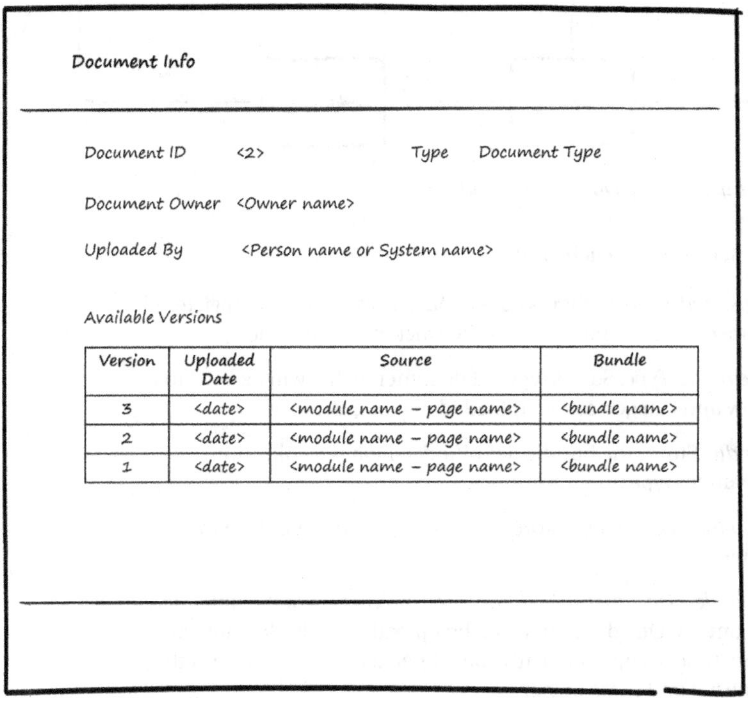

Figure 4-9. *Uploaded document information*

Documents Module Entities

Now that you've seen the use-cases and wireframes for the Documents module, it's time to see the entities used by the Documents module to store the document information. Figure 4-10 shows the entities and relations between them.

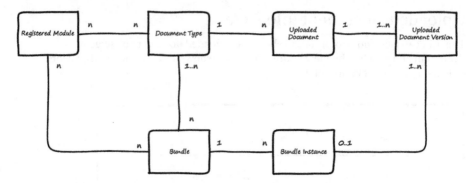

Figure 4-10. *Entities for the Documents module*

Here is a description for each entity:

- *Registered Module*: Stores data about the modules that registered themselves to be managed by the Documents module.

- *Document Type*: Stores types of documents that will be used to allow and categorize the uploaded documents.

- *Bundle*: Stores the bundle definition, which is a collection of document types.

- *Uploaded Document*: Stores the uploaded documents in the system.

- *Uploaded Document Version*: Stores the version of the uploaded document. One document can be uploaded multiple times, and every time it's uploaded, it's considered a new version if it is the same file and same owner.

- *Bundle Instance*: Stores the instances of the bundles uploaded to the system. When a bundle is required to be uploaded, the user will upload documents with the types defined in the bundle. This is considered a bundle instance.

The relations between these entities can be summarized like this:

- The Registered Module can support multiple document types, and multiple Registered Modules can support one document type.

- The Registered Module can support multiple bundles, and a bundle can be supported by multiple registered modules.

- The Bundle definition contains one or more document types.

- An uploaded document can have multiple versions.

- A Bundle instance contains uploaded documents with specific versions.

Use of the Documents Module by Other Modules

The Documents module accepts other modules to be plugged into it so that the documents for other modules can be managed by the Documents module.

Modules can be plugged into the Documents module using the Register Module use-case. In order to be registered, they should implement the Register Module interface and they should have documents types and bundles stored in the format supported by the Document module. The interface needs the module to be registered to be able to answer the following questions, and the answer will be used to fill the entities, as described:

- *Who are you?* The answer to this question will be saved in the Registered Module entity.

- *What document types do you use?* The answer to this question will be saved in Document Type entity.

- *What bundles do you use?* The answer to this question will be saved in the Bundle entity.

After a module is plugged into the Lookups module, it will be able to use the Get Types or Get Bundles use-case to get the types and bundle definition if updated by the admin. In addition, it can use the Get Uploaded Documents use-case to return the uploaded documents for a bundle instance.

Summary

This chapter discussed the Documents module, including what document types and bundles are, why documents are required, and use-cases for the Documents module. I also showed wireframes for the screens and explained the entities and their relations. The last section showed how other modules could use the Documents module.

CHAPTER 5

■ ■ ■

Persons Module

Software systems deal with people (persons). *Persons* can be users, customers, employees, vendor contacts, or any other role a person can perform. This means every software system should support the ability to manage persons' data. In this chapter, I discuss the Persons module. The Persons module's main functionality is to enable software systems to manage persons' data and prevent the duplication of persons in the systems.

After finishing this chapter, you will be able to answer the following questions:

- Why do you need to store persons' information?

- What information is to be stored about persons?

- How does the UI for the Persons module look?

Importance of Persons' Information

As mentioned, any software system will need to store information about persons, and persons play different roles in a system. A person can be a user of the system, employee in the organization, customer, vendor, or something else depending on the business of the organization. In addition, one person may play many different roles in the system, and that's why the system must not duplicate any person's information but should manage it centrally. Roles can be added to the person without duplicating the person's information.

The Persons module is used to manage persons' information, which may include the following:

- Personal information

- Contact information (home telephone, mobile number, e-mail, website URL, address, and so on)

- Relationships between persons in the system (for example, son, father, wife, husband, and so forth)

© Mohamed Farouk 2017
M. Farouk, *Infrastructure Software Modules for Enterprises*,
DOI 10.1007/978-1-4842-3021-3_5

Persons Module Use-Cases

Figure 5-1 shows use-cases for the Persons module. Actors for these use-cases are the user who has permission to manage persons and system modules. A system module can be a business module or infrastructure module that needs to retrieve persons' information.

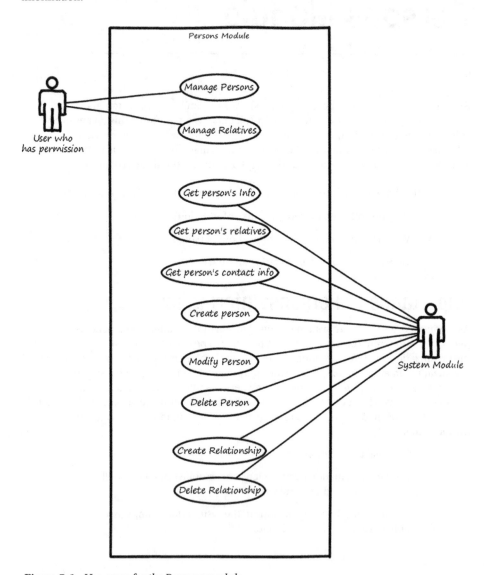

Figure 5-1. *Use-cases for the Persons module*

Here is a description for each use-case:

- *Manage persons*: This use-case is used to view, add, modify, and delete persons and their contact information.

- *Manage relatives*: This use-case is used to view, add, modify, and delete relatives for persons.

- *Get person's info*: This use-case is used to return information about a person to other modules when they ask for it.

- *Get person's contact info*: This use-case is used to return contact information of a person to other modules when they ask for it.

- *Get person's relatives*: This use-case is used to return a list of relatives for a person (and their relationship to this person) to other modules when they ask for them.

- *Create person*: This use-case is used to enable other modules to create a new person.

- *Modify person*: This use-case is used to enable other modules to modify an existing person's data.

- *Delete person*: This use-case is used to enable other modules to delete an existing person.

- *Create relationship*: This use-case is used to enable other modules to create a relationship between existing two persons.

- *Delete relationship*: This use-case is used to enable other modules to delete an existing relationship between two persons.

Persons Module Wireframes

This section shows high-level wireframe screens for the Persons module. The UI flow is shown in Figure 5-2.

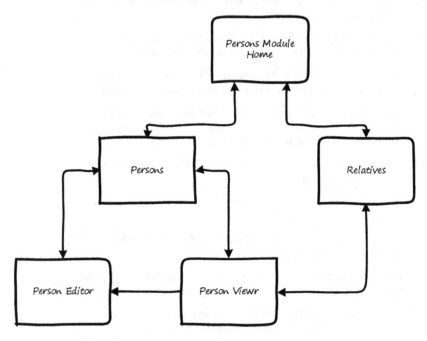

Figure 5-2. *UI flow for the Persons module*

From the home page of the Persons module, the user can navigate to the Persons page, where they can manage persons (search, view, add, modify, delete). The user can add and modify a person's information by navigating to the Person Editor page and can view a person's information by navigating to the Person Viewer page. It is also possible from the home page to navigate to the Relatives page, where the user can view and search persons with relationships to other persons. In the rest of this section, I go through what these pages look like.

Persons Page

This page is used to manage persons. Users can view, add, edit, and delete a person in the system. It also shows the user which module created this person. A person can be created either from Persons module or from other business modules. Figure 5-3 shows a wireframe for listing persons.

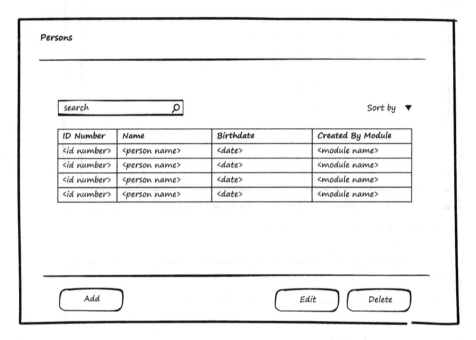

Persons

ID Number	Name	Birthdate	Created By Module
<id number>	<person name>	<date>	<module name>
<id number>	<person name>	<date>	<module name>
<id number>	<person name>	<date>	<module name>
<id number>	<person name>	<date>	<module name>

search

Sort by ▼

Add   Edit   Delete

Figure 5-3. *Manage persons*

Person Editor Page

Figures 5-4 through 5-6 show wireframes for the Person Editor page, which can be used for editing or adding person. This page has three tabs: Basic Info, Contact Info, and Relatives.

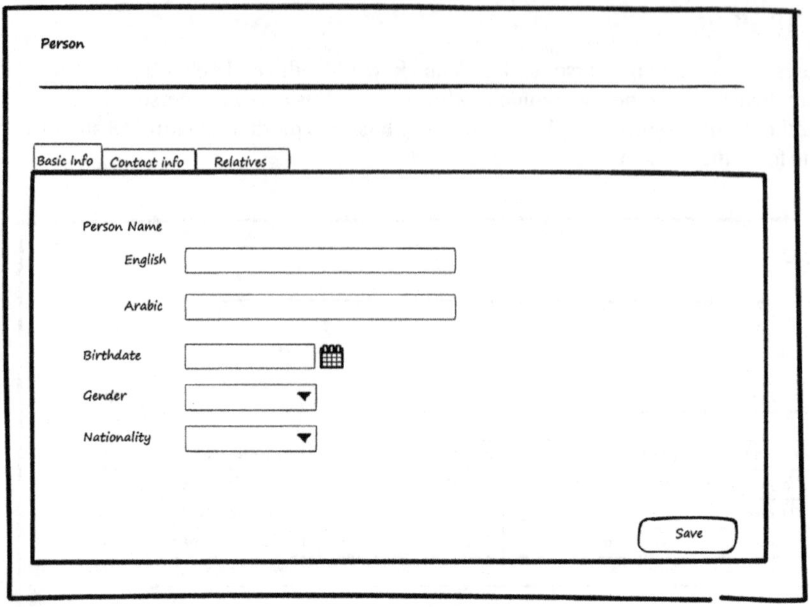

Figure 5-4. *Edit person: basic information*

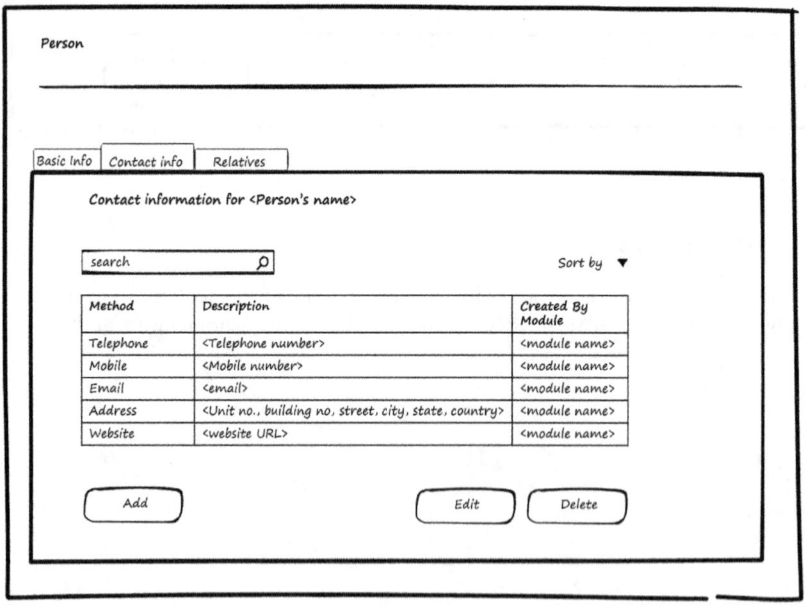

Figure 5-5. *Edit person: contact information*

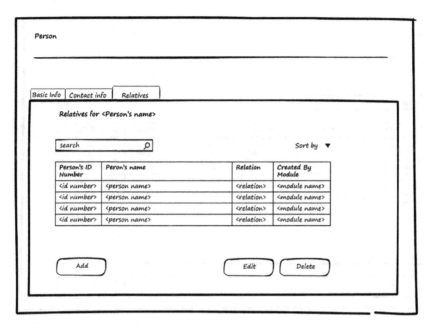

Figure 5-6. *Edit person: relatives*

This page will depend on the Localization module to support entering a person's name in the supported languages.

Relatives Page

This page is used to manage the relationships between persons. Users can view, add, edit, and delete relationships between two persons. Relationships can be created either from the Persons module or from other business modules. Figure 5-7 shows a wireframe for listing relationships between persons.

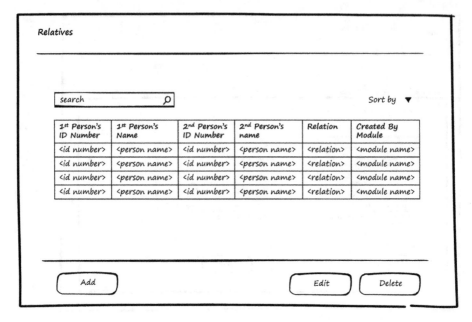

Figure 5-7. *Manage relationships*

Persons Module Entities

Now that you've seen use-cases and wireframes for the Persons module, it's time to see the entities used by the Persons module to store the persons' information. Figure 5-8 shows the entities and relations between them.

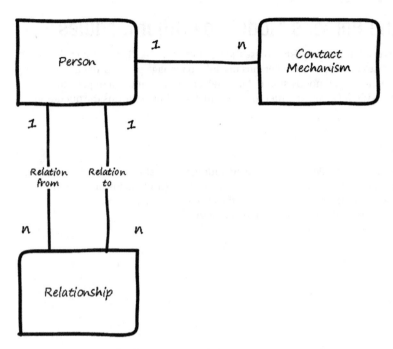

Figure 5-8. Entities for the Persons module

Here is a description for each entity:

- *Person*: Stores basic information for the person.

- *Contact Mechanism*: Stores contact information for the person.

- *Relationship*: Stores the relationship between two persons. The relationship has two directions (for example, if person P1 is *father* for person P2, then P2 is *son* for P1) and it is stored once. There is no need to duplicate the storage because the second direction of the relation can be inferred.

The relations between these entities can be summarized as below:

- A person can have multiple contact mechanisms.

- A person can participate in multiple relationships with other persons.

Use of the Persons Module by Other Modules

Other modules don't need to register to use the Persons module. They can start directly using the use-cases provided by the Persons module to manage persons' data.

For the use-cases that modify stored data, the Persons module will request the calling module to identify itself in order to track which module performs the operation.

Summary

This chapter discussed the Persons module, including why to store persons' information, and what information is to be stored. It discussed use-cases for Persons module and showed wireframes for the screens. I covered the entities and their relations and discussed how other modules could use the Persons module.

CHAPTER 6

■ ■ ■

Organization Structure Module

Every organization consists of departments (suborganizations), and these departments are organized into a hierarchy. Each department has *positions* inside it to be filled by employees. Positions also are organized into a hierarchy called a *reporting hierarchy*. Organizations and positions are required for giving permissions to employees on the functionalities in the system. This means every software system should support the ability to define organizations and positions. The Organization Structure module's main functionality is to enable software systems to manage the definition of the organization hierarchy and the positions reporting hierarchy.

After finishing this chapter, you will be able to answer the following questions:

- What are organization hierarchies, positions, and reporting hierarchies?

- What kind of information is to be stored for an organization hierarchy and reporting hierarchy?

- What does the UI for the Organization Structure module look like?

An organization is a group of people. In business, it is a group of positions and employees to fill these positions. An organization may be an Enterprise, Directorate, Department, Section, or Committee. An organization can contain suborganizations. For example, Department will have employees working in it and may consist of Sections, with each Section having employees working in it.

The components of the Organization Structure are as follows:

- *Organization hierarchy*: This refers to the relations between parts of the organization. In most cases, a suborganization can be part of one organization, and one organization can consist of multiple suborganizations.

- *Positions*: These are the jobs in the organization. An employee fills the position for a period until they retire, quit, or move. Then another employee fills the position for another period, and so on.

© Mohamed Farouk 2017

M. Farouk, *Infrastructure Software Modules for Enterprises*,
DOI 10.1007/978-1-4842-3021-3_6

- *Reporting hierarchy*: Refers to the relations between positions in the organization, including which positions reports to which positions. In most cases, a position reports to only one position. However, in some cases, a position can report to multiple positions—for example, when an employee has a manager and supervisor.

Back in Chapter 1, Figures 1-6 and 1-7 show examples of organization hierarchy and reporting hierarchy.

Organization Structure Module Use-Cases

Figure 6-1 shows use-cases for the Organization Structure module. Actors for these use-cases are the user, who has permission to manage persons, and system modules, which may be business modules or infrastructure modules that need to retrieve Organization Structure's info.

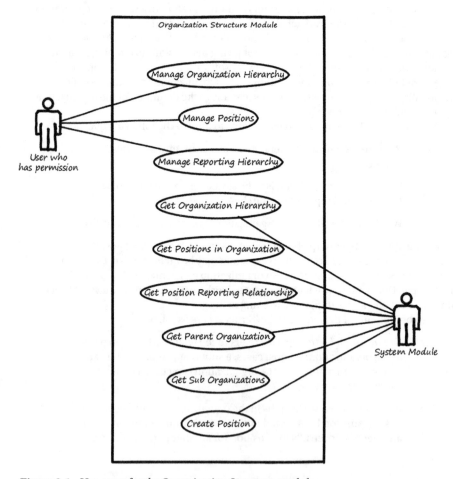

Figure 6-1. *Use-cases for the Organization Structure module*

Here is a description for each use-case:

- *Manage organization hierarchy*: This use-case is used to search, view, add, modify, and delete organizations and the relations that build the hierarchy.

- *Manage positions*: This use-case is used to search, view, add, modify, and delete positions in the organizations.

- *Manage reporting hierarchy*: This use-case is used to search, view, add, modify, and delete reporting relation between positions in the organizations.

- *Get organization hierarchy*: This use-case is used to return the organization and all suborganizations under it according to the requested deep level.

- *Get positions in organization*: This use-case is used to return positions in one organization only, without its suborganizations.

- *Get position reporting relationship*: This use-case is used to return the positions that the requested position reports to in addition to the reporting type.

- *Get parent organization*: This use-case is used to return the parent organization for a certain organization.

- *Get suborganizations*: This use-case is used to return organizations under a specific organization.

- *Create position*: This use-case is used to enable other modules to create a new position in an organization.

Organization Structure Module Wireframes

This section shows high-level wireframe screens for the Organization Structure module. The UI flow is shown in Figure 6-2.

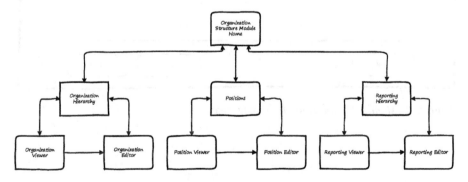

Figure 6-2. *UI flow for the Organization Structure module*

From the home page of the Organization Structure module, the user can navigate to the Organization Hierarchy page where they can manage organizations (search, view, add, modify, delete, and specify relations). The user can manage this information by navigating to the Organization Editor page and view organization information by navigating to Organization Viewer page. The user can also navigate from the home page to the Positions page and manage positions (search, view, add, modify, and delete) and manage this information by navigating to the Position Editor page. The user can also view position information by navigating to the Position Viewer page and can navigate from the home page to the Reporting Hierarchy page to manage reporting relationships among positions (search, view, add, modify, and delete). The user can manage this information by navigating to the Reporting Editor page. The user can view relationships between positions by navigating to the Reporting Viewer page. In the rest of this section, you will see how these pages look.

Organization Hierarchy Page

This page is used to manage organizations. The user can view, add, edit, and delete organizations in the system. Figure 6-3 shows a wireframe for listing organizations.

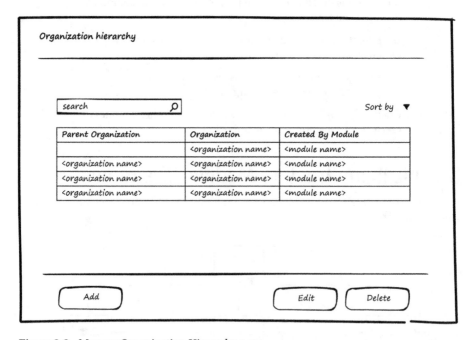

Figure 6-3. *Manage Organization Hierarchy page*

Organization Editor Page

Figures 6-4 and 6-5 show wireframes for the Organization Editor page, which can be used for editing or adding organization. This page consists of two tabs: Basic Info and Contact Info.

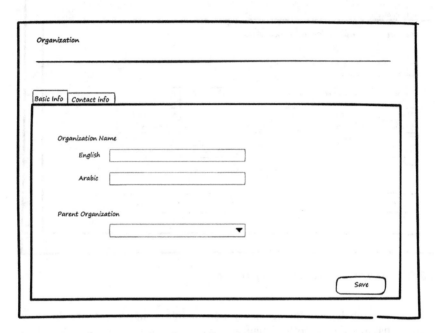

Figure 6-4. *Edit Organization: basic information*

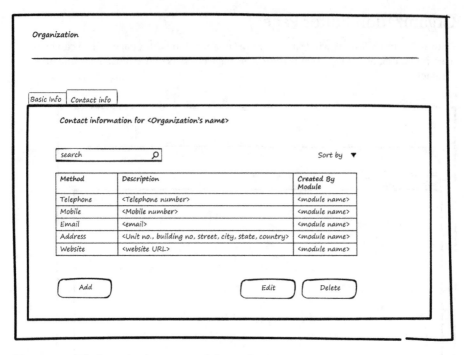

Figure 6-5. *Edit Organization: contact information*

The Basic Info tab depends on the Localization module to support entering the organization's name in the supported languages.

Positions Page

This page is used to manage positions. The user can view, add, edit, and delete positions in the system. Figure 6-6 shows a wireframe for listing positions.

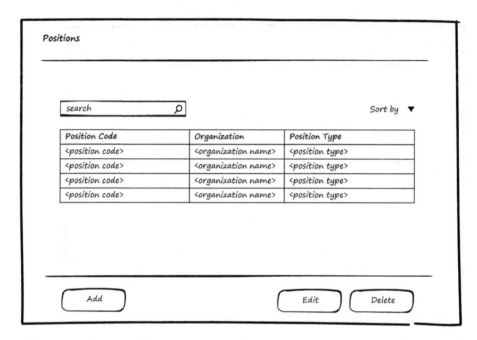

Figure 6-6. *Manage positions*

Position Editor Page

In Figure 6-7, you can see a wireframe for the Position Editor page, which can be used for editing or adding positions.

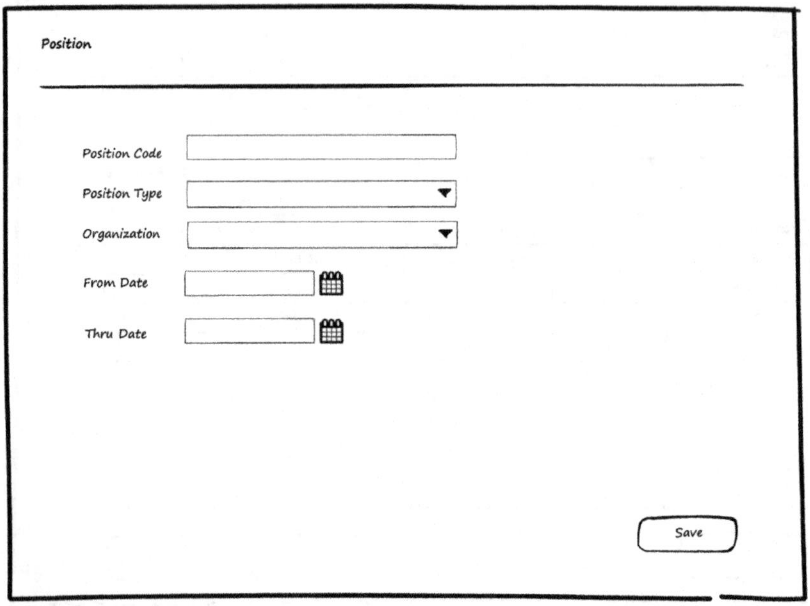

Figure 6-7. *Edit position*

Reporting Hierarchy Page

This page is used to manage reporting hierarchy among positions. The user can view, add, edit, and delete reporting relationships in the system. Figure 6-8 shows a wireframe for listing reporting relationships. One position can report to multiple positions with different reporting types.

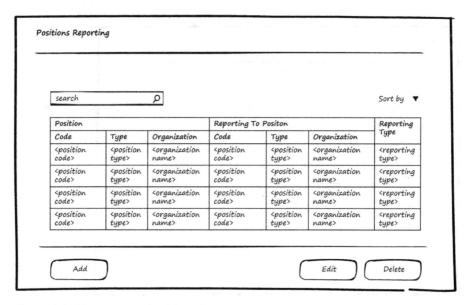

Figure 6-8. *Manage reporting hierarchy*

Reporting Editor Page

Figure 6-9 shows a wireframe for the Reporting Editor page, which can be used for editing or adding reporting relationships between two positions. To select a position, the user first chooses the organization from the first drop-down list and then selects the position from the second drop-down list. The second drop-down list displays the position codes concatenated with the position types.

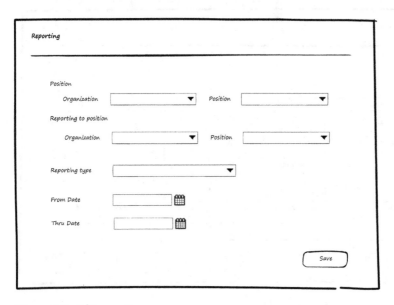

Figure 6-9. *Edit reporting*

Organization Structure Module Entities

Now that you've seen use-cases and wireframes for the Organization Structure module, it's time to see the entities used by the Organization Structure module to store the Organization Structure's information. Figure 6-10 shows the entities and the relations between them.

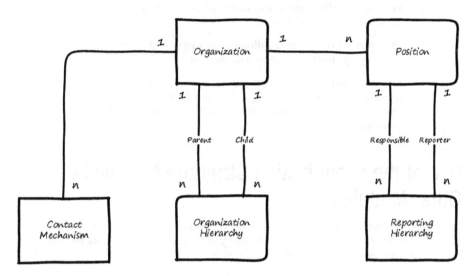

Figure 6-10. *Entities for the Organization Structure module*

Here is a description for each entity:

- *Organization*: Stores basic information about the organization.

- *Contact mechanism*: Stores contact information for the organization.

- *Organization hierarchy*: Stores the relationships between the organizations. The organization can have multiple organizations under it in the hierarchy.

- *Position*: Stores information about the position.

- *Reporting hierarchy*: Stores the reporting relationships between positions.

The relations between these entities can be summarized like this:

- Organization can have multiple contact mechanisms.

- Organization can be part of a parent organization in the organization hierarchy, and one organization can have multiple organizations under it in the organization hierarchy.

- Position must be in one organization, and Organization can contain multiple positions.

- Organization can contain multiple positions with the same position type but the position code must differ.

- Position can report to multiple positions (one of them will be the main or default reporting) with different reporting types. One position can be responsible for multiple positions with different reporting types.

Use of the Organization Structure Module by Other Modules

Other modules don't need to register to use the Organization Structure module. They can start directly using the use-cases provided by the Organization Structure module to manage organization structure. These use-cases are as follows:

- Get organization hierarchy

- Get positions in organization

- Get position reporting relationship

- Get parent organization

- Get suborganizations

- Create position

For the use-cases that modify stored data, the Organization Structure module will request the calling module to identify itself in order to track which module performs the operation.

Summary

This chapter discussed the Organization Structure module, including organization hierarchy, positions, and reporting hierarchy, and the use-cases for the Organization Structure module. Wireframes for the screens were shown, and you saw the entities and their relations. In the last section, I talked about how other modules could use the Organization Structure module.

CHAPTER 7

■ ■ ■

Authentication Module

People (persons) who use a software system need to be authenticated in order to be known to the system and to allow the system to track their operations. This means every software system should support the ability to identify who is the person currently using it. There are many methods for authentication and identification. The Authentication module's main functionality is to enable software systems to authenticate the persons who use the system to identify them. It does this by associating persons with user accounts and managing how they will be identified.

After finishing this chapter, you will be able to answer the following questions:

- What is authentication?

- What information is to be stored for authenticating users?

- How does the UI for the Authentication module look?

A person who is stored in the system and managed by the Persons module can access the system and perform functionalities based on the permissions given to them. In order for a person to access the system, they need to be represented by a user in the system. Therefore, every person will have one user account to enable them to log in to the system and be identified.

Authentication is the process of identifying the user (or person) to the system. By providing information to the system, the system will know who the user (or person) is whose information is provided. The information to be provided to the system to authenticate the user may be, for example, username and password, fingerprint, eye print, or physical token.

The system should first register the user with this identification information in order to do the authentication later. Registration can be done using information that the person knows (such as password, username and password, e-mail and password, or mobile number and password), physical objects the person has access to (device, ID card, physical token), or unique attributes of the person (fingerprint, voice, eye, or face). The registration information may also involve a combination of these things.

Based on the registration methods, the system will allow the person to select the authentication method and will compare the entered information with the registered information to authenticate and identify the user.

© Mohamed Farouk 2017

M. Farouk, *Infrastructure Software Modules for Enterprises*,

DOI 10.1007/978-1-4842-3021-3_7

In addition to identification, the user may be allowed to use the system only at specific times. For example, the user may use the system only during working days, and not on weekends. Therefore, every user could have a login schedule to log in to the system. Moreover, user access to the system may be blocked by deactivating the user, which means changing the user's account status from active to inactive.

Authentication is about identifying the user by the supported authentication mechanisms and allowing them to access the system based on the login schedule and user status of active or inactive.

Required Information for Authentication

The Authentication module will need to store the following information:

- *User information*: Who the person is that this user represents and what the status of the user is (active or inactive).

- *Login schedule*: When the user can log in to the system.

- *Authentication mechanisms*: Based on the supported mechanism by the system, the Authentication module will need to store the information that will allow authenticating the user—for example, username and password, fingerprint, eye print, or other method.

Authentication Module Use-Cases

Figure 7-1 shows the use-cases for Authentication module. Actors for these use-cases are the user who has permission to manage users and a system module, which can be a business module or infrastructure module that needs to authenticate or create users.

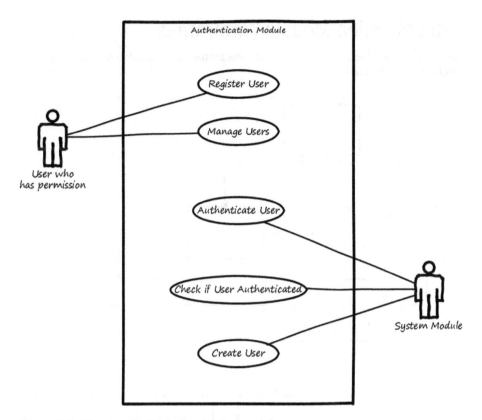

Figure 7-1. *Use-cases for the Authentication module*

Here is a description for each use-case:

- *Register users*: This use-case is used to add new users, specify login schedules, and specify authentication mechanisms for the user.

- *Manage users*: This use-case is used to search, view, add, modify, and delete users.

- *Authenticate user*: This use-case is used to allow identifying and authenticating the user based on information provided to log in to the system and the information stored about the user in the Authentication module.

- *Check if user authenticated*: This use-case is used to inform its actor if a certain user is authenticated or not.

- *Create user*: This use-case is used to enable other modules to add new users, specify login schedules, and specify authentication mechanisms for the user.

Authentication Module Wireframes

This section shows high-level wireframe screens for the Authentication module. The UI flow is shown in Figure 7-2.

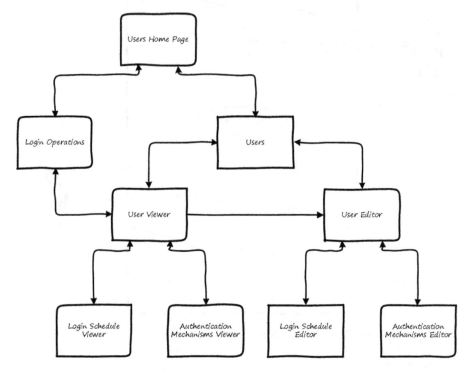

Figure 7-2. *UI flow for the Authentication module*

From the home page of the Authentication module, the user can navigate to Login Operations page where they can view and search the login attempts for users. The user can also navigate to the Users page to manage users (search, view, add, modify, and delete). The user can manage this information by navigating to the User Editor page, where they can specify the login schedule by navigating to the Login Schedule Editor page. To specify the authentication mechanisms, the user can go to the Authentication Mechanisms Editor page. Also from the Users page the user can view the information about the user by going to the User Viewer page where they can navigate to the Login Schedule Viewer page and the Authentication Mechanisms Viewer page.

In the rest of this section, we will see what these pages look like.

Users Page

This page is used to manage users. The user can search, view, add, edit, and delete users in the system. Figure 7-3 shows a wireframe for listing users.

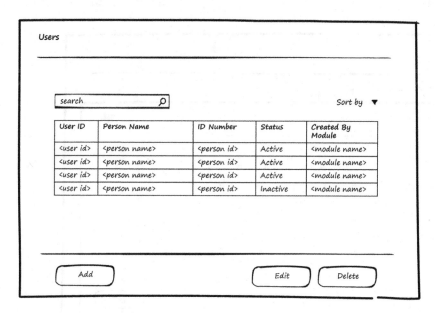

Figure 7-3. *Manage users*

User Editor Page

In Figure 7-4, you can see the wireframe for the User Editor page, which can be used for editing or adding users. A user is associated with one person and can be active or inactive.

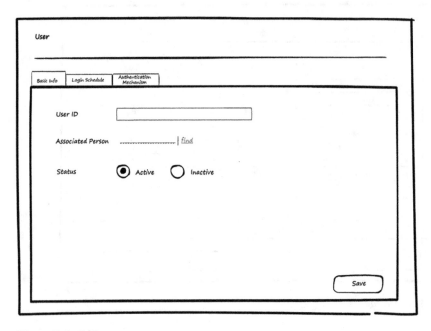

Figure 7-4. *Edit user*

Login Schedule Editor Page

In Figure 7-5, you can see a wireframe for the Login Schedule Editor page, which can be used for specifying a login schedule for the user. The user can be allowed to log in to the system on specific days, and for each day, the user can have multiple periods for login.

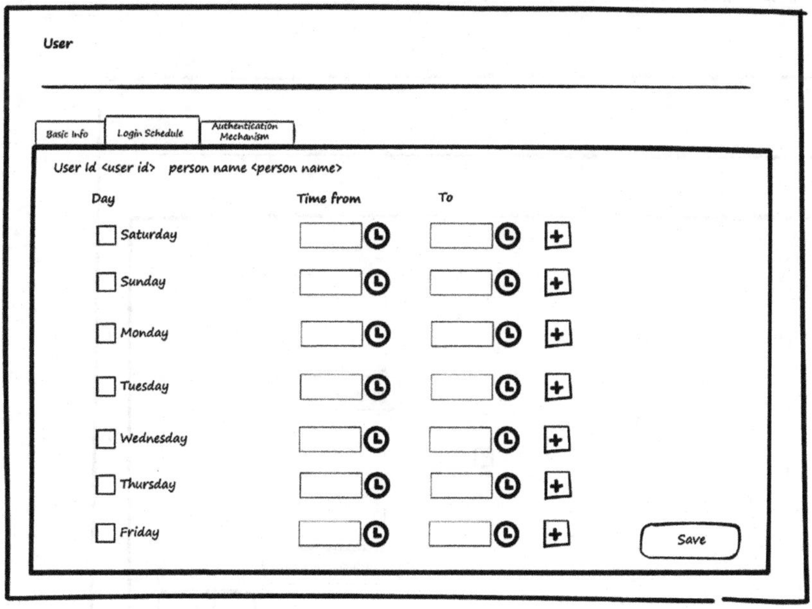

Figure 7-5. Edit Login schedule

Authentication Mechanisms Editor Page

Figure 7-6 shows wireframe for the Authentication Mechanisms Editor page, which can be used to select authentication methods for the user. A user can be allowed to log in to the system with multiple methods, including biometric identifications. To use biometric identifications, the system will need to capture the fingerprint and/or eye print. The system will allow the user to use these methods to log in to the system from the login page.

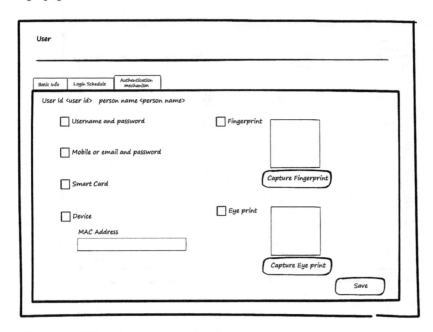

Figure 7-6. *Edit authentication mechanisms*

Figure 7-7 shows an example for the login page. The login page allows the user to select the login mechanism from the mechanisms supported by the system. When the user select a method, the system will open the page that supports the login with the selected mechanism and validate the user based on the assigned login mechanisms for them.

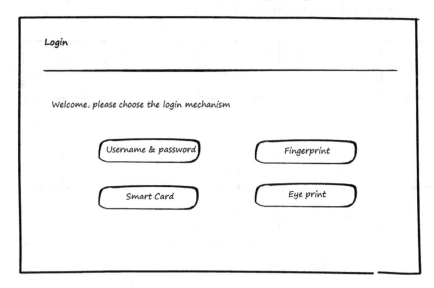

Figure 7-7. Login page

Login Operations Page

This page is used to view information about attempts to log in to the system. The user can search and see when the operation is done, by what mechanism, and whether it failed or succeeded (if failed, the user will be able to see the reason). Figure 7-8 shows a wireframe for listing login operations.

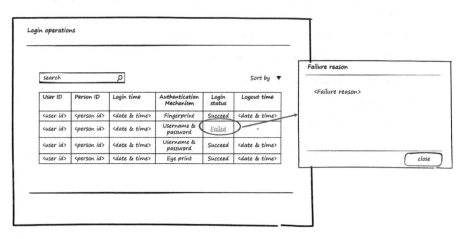

Figure 7-8. List of login operations

Authentication Module Entities

Now that you've seen use-cases and wireframes for the Authentication module, let's look at the entities used by the Authentication module to store users' information. Figure 7-9 shows the entities and relations between them.

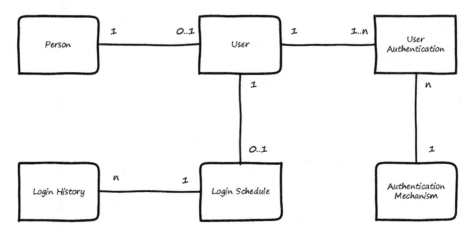

Figure 7-9. *Entities for the Authentication module*

Here is a description for each entity:

- *User*: Stores basic information about the user.

- *User Authentication*: Stores authentication mechanisms for the users.

- *Login Schedule*: Stores the login schedule for the users.

- *Login History*: Stores information about how users have logged in to the system.

The relations between these entities can be summarized as below:

- User can be associated to one person only.

- Person may have one or no user.

- User can have one or more authentication mechanisms.

- User can have only one login schedule.

- Multiple login operations can be done based on the user login schedule.

Use of the Authentication module by Other Modules

Other modules don't need to register to use the Authentication module. They can start directly using the use-cases provided by the Authentication module to authenticate users. These use-cases include the following:

- Authenticate users

- Check if user authenticated

- Create user

For the use-cases that modify stored data, the Authentication module will request the calling module to identify itself in order to track which module performs the operation.

Summary

This chapter discussed the Authentication module, including user info, login schedule, and authentication mechanisms. I discussed the use-cases and showed wireframes for the screens. You were introduced to the entities and their relations, and you saw how other modules could use the Authentication module.

CHAPTER 8

■ ■ ■

Authorization Module

Persons who use a software system must not perform actions unless they are given permission to perform those actions. In addition, they must not retrieve data unless they have permission to view that data. This means every software system should be flexible in managing the permissions for its users. It should be easy for the system administrator to deny or allow users to perform actions or retrieve data from the system. The Authorization module's main functionality is to enable software systems to manage users' permissions on functionality and data.

After finishing this chapter, you will be able to answer the following questions:

- What are services, roles, and groups?

- What is authorization?

- Why do you need authorization?

- How should you store authorization data?

- What does the UI for the Authorization module look like?

Let's cover a few definitions before we get started. A *service* in the context of this book is a functionality the user can perform in the system. This may include adding, deleting, updating, viewing, and searching for data in the system, or filling and sending e-application forms.

A service can be mapped to UI elements. For example, if we have a service called Add Employee it would be mapped to the Add button in the UI. A service called View Employee Salary would be mapped to the data section on the UI that represents the employee salary.

A *role* is a behavior that can be acted by an entity and is used to enable some entities to behave in the system in a certain way. A role can be played by position, organization, user, or group.

Let's say we have some departments in the organization that acts as committees of a certain type (for example, a stocktaking committee). Or maybe we have some employees in a department who act as approvers for a certain applications type, or perhaps the users of the system can be categorized as visitors and employees.

© Mohamed Farouk 2017
M. Farouk, *Infrastructure Software Modules for Enterprises*,
DOI 10.1007/978-1-4842-3021-3_8

This act called the role is a behavior that an entity can be assigned to play. The role can have specific permissions or can perform predefined tasks in the system.

A *group* is a combination of entities of different types and is used to make it easier to manage permission in the system by combining entities and then using that group to define permissions. A group's members can also perform predefined tasks in the system.

Authorization is giving permission to users of the system to perform functionalities in the system and to view or retrieve data from the system.

There are two types of authorization:

- *Authorization to perform a functionality*: Enables users to perform a set of functionalities in the system (based on the permissions given to them)

- *Authorization to access data*: Enables users to view a set of data (based on the permission given to them) and perform a set of functionality that they are authorized to perform

This chapter focuses on authorization for functionality. Permission for a functionality can be one of the following values:

- Allow

- Deny

- None

By default, users are denied all functionalities in the system. They can access functionality and data only if they are given *allow* permission for it.

Importance of Authorization

Users play different roles in the system. Not all functionality can be done by all users. Multiple factors affect what functionalities the user is allowed to perform in the system:

- The roles played by the user

- The position the user is hired into

- The type of the user's position

- The organization the user works in

- The groups the user is a member of

Based on those factors, the organization may give permission to the user to perform functionalities in the system.

The goal of authorization is to allow managing the service (functionalities) in the system and to provide access to these services to users who should be able to perform these functionalities and to deny access to the services for users who should not be able to perform these functionalities.

Authorization Module Use-Cases

Figure 8-1 shows use-cases for Authorization module. Actors for these use-cases are the user who has permission to manage users and a system module, which can be a business module or infrastructure module that needs to check authorization for a user.

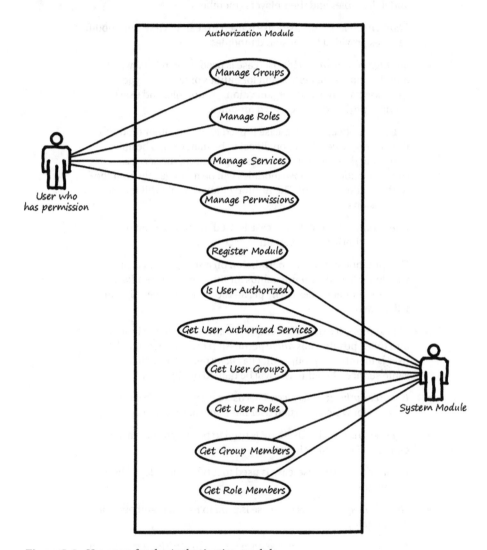

Figure 8-1. *Use-cases for the Authorization module*

Here is a description for each use-case:

- *Manage groups*: This use-case is used to search, view, add, modify, and delete groups and their members.

- *Manage roles*: This use-case is used to search, view, add, modify, and delete roles and their players (members).

- *Manage services*: This use-case is used to search, view, and modify services provided by registered modules.

- *Manage permissions*: This use-case is used to search, view, add, modify, and delete permission for entities of different types (position type, position, organization, group, role, and user) on services provided by registered modules.

- *Register module*: This use-case is used to enable other modules that have services (functionalities) to be managed to be able to register their information. After registration, the services (functionalities) for those modules will be manageable from the Authorization module. The Authorization module will manage permission on these services.

- *Is user authorized*: This use-case is used to inform its actor if a user is authorized on a certain service or not.

  Computation of the final permission on a service for a user will depend on the memberships for this user. If any entity a user is member of has a *deny* permission, the final permission will be deny.

  For example, if a user is an employee and works in position X and this X position has *allow* permission on a service, but the user is member of group Y that has *deny* permission on the same service, then the user will be denied on the service.

- *Get user authorized services*: This use-case is used to return services for which a certain user has *allow* permissions.

- *Get user groups*: This use-case is used to return groups having a certain user member in them.

- *Get user roles*: This use-case is used to return roles played by a certain user.

- *Get role members*: This use-case is used to return members of a certain role.

- *Get group members*: This use-case is used to return members of a certain group.

Authorization Module Wireframes

This section shows high-level wireframe screens for the Authorization module. The UI flow is shown in Figure 8-2.

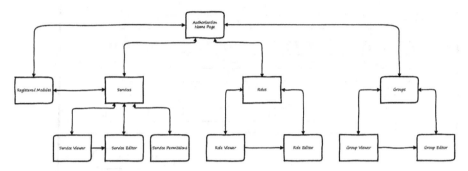

Figure 8-2. *UI flow for the Authorization module*

From the home page of the Authorization module, the user can navigate to the Registered Modules page to view and search the registered modules. The user can navigate to the Services page to manage the services of a selected module and can see service details by going to the Service Viewer page. To edit the service, the user can go to the Service Editor page, and to manage permission on a service they can navigate to the Service Permissions page where they can allow/deny entities on the services. The user can also navigate to the Services page directly from the Authorization module home page.

To manage groups, the user will navigate from the home page to the Groups page. To view group information, the user can go to the Group Viewer page. Modifying the group can be done by navigating to the Group Editor page.

To manage roles, the user goes from the home page to the Roles page, and to view role information they can go to the Role Viewer page. Modifying the role can be done by navigating to the Role Editor page.

The rest of this section discusses what these pages look like.

Registered Modules Page

When other modules are registered (plugged) into the Authorization module, they will appear in the Registered Modules page. From this page, the user will be able to manage the services provided by these modules. Figure 8-3 shows a wireframe for listing the registered modules.

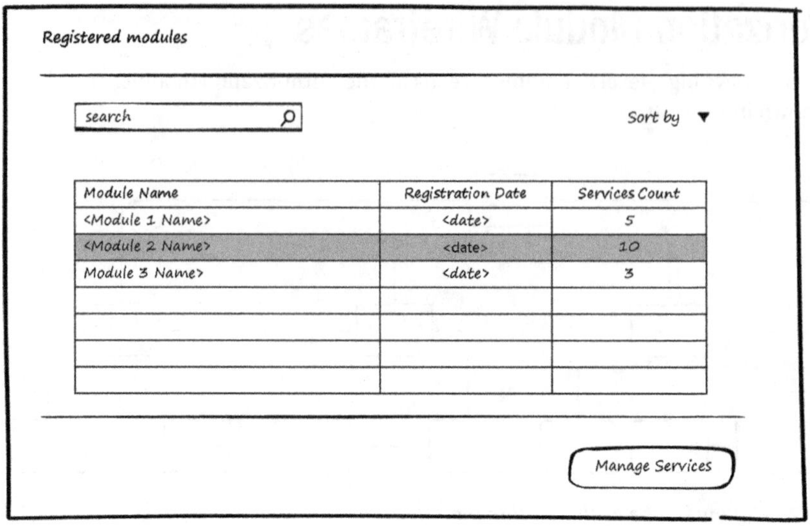

Figure 8-3. *Registered modules to be managed by the Authorization module*

Services Page

This page is used to manage services for a registered module. Users can search, view, add, edit, and delete services in the system. Figure 8-4 shows a wireframe for listing services.

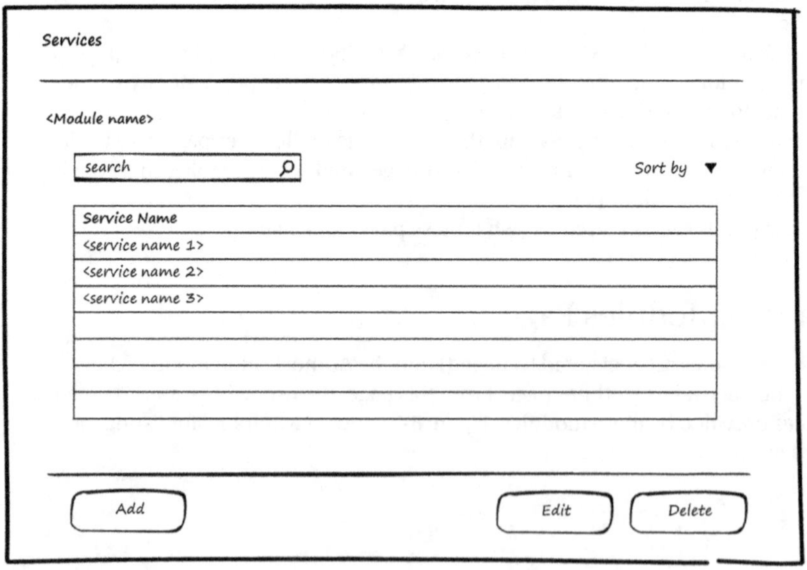

Figure 8-4. *Manage services*

Service Editor Page

In Figure 8-5, you can see a wireframe for the Service Editor page, which can be used for editing or adding a service. The Service Editor page contains two tabs: Basic Info and Permissions.

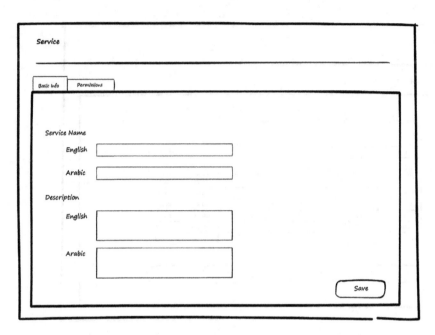

Figure 8-5. *Edit service: basic info*

The Basic Info tab will depend on the Localization module to support entering the name and description of the service in the supported languages.

Service Permissions Page

The Service Permissions page is the second tab in the Service Editor page. This page is used to manage permissions on the service. Users can search, view, add, edit, and delete permissions. Figure 8-6 shows a wireframe for listing services.

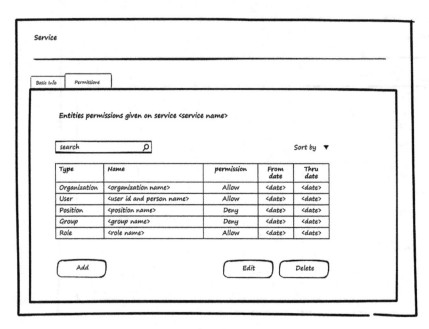

Figure 8-6. *Edit Service: Manage permissions*

The Permission Editor page shown in Figure 8-7 is used to add or edit permission on the selected service. The user can choose the entity type (which can be any of the following: Organization, Position Type, Position, Role, User, or Group) and then find the entity they want to give it permission. Permission can be Allow, Deny, or None. In addition, a period for this permission should be specified.

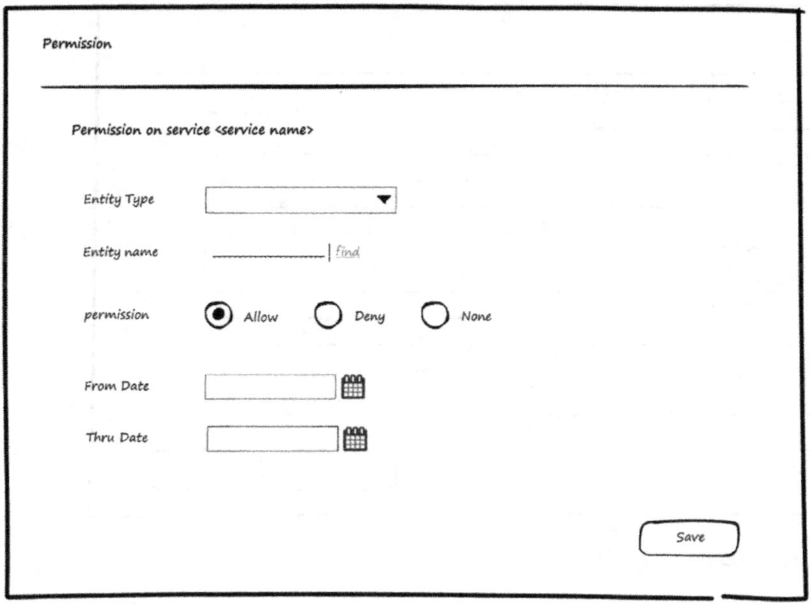

Figure 8-7. Edit permission

Groups Page

This page is used to manage groups. Users can search, view, add, edit, and delete groups in the system. Figure 8-8 shows a wireframe for listing groups.

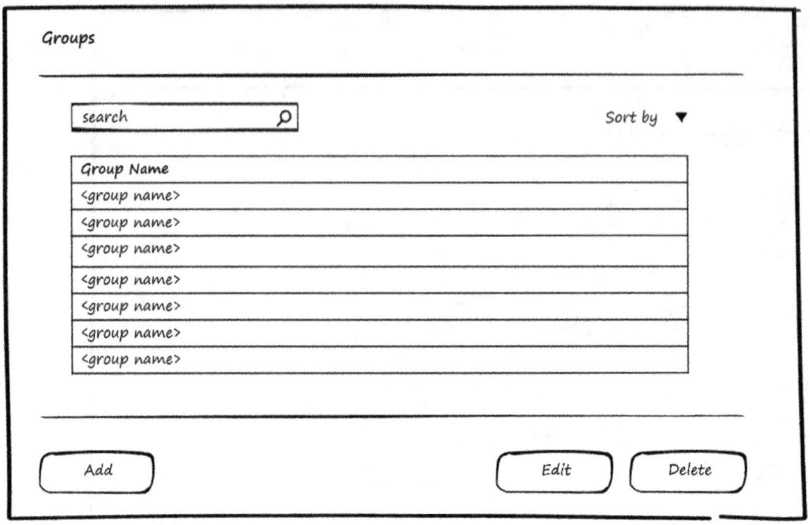

Figure 8-8. *Manage groups*

Group Editor Page

Figures 8-9 and 8-10 show wireframes for the Group Editor page, which can be used for editing or adding groups. This page has two tabs: Basic Info and Members.

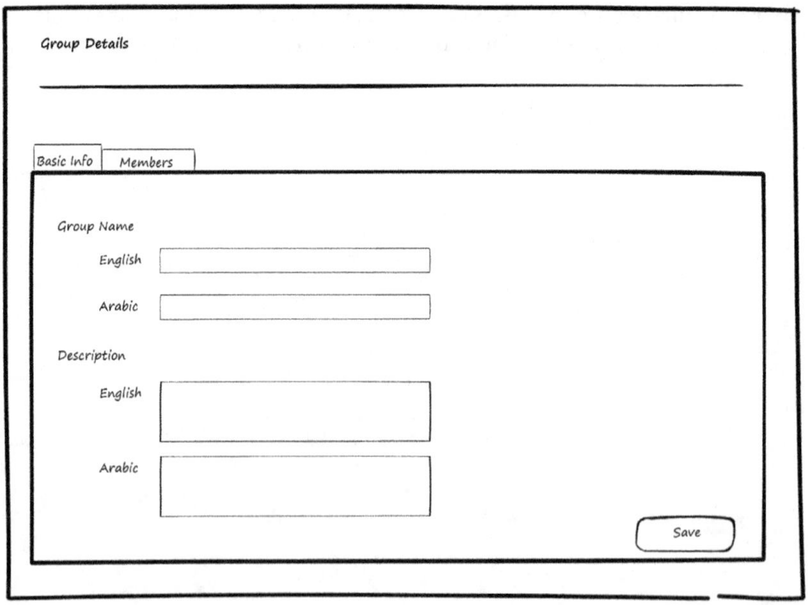

Figure 8-9. *Edit group: basic info*

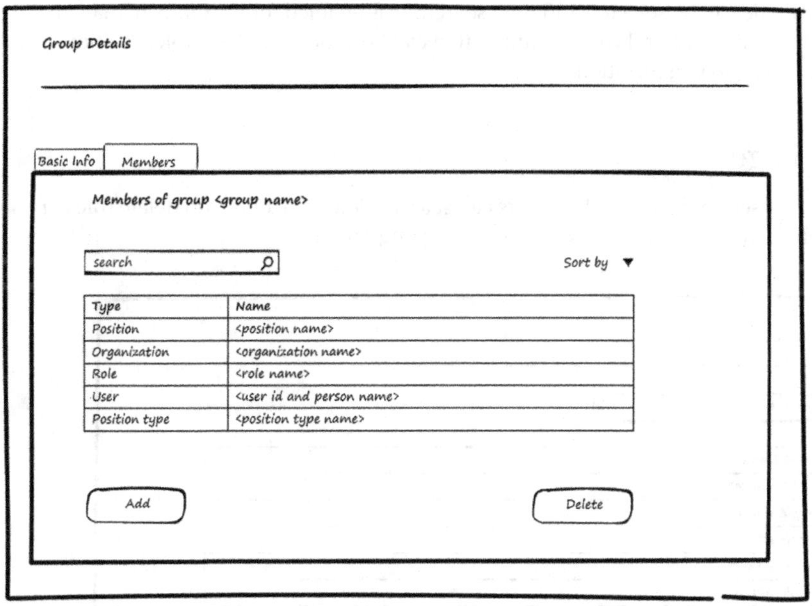

Figure 8-10. *Edit group: Members*

In the Members tab, it's possible to add members to the group from different entity types. A wireframe for the page to find a member to be added to the group is shown in Figure 8-11.

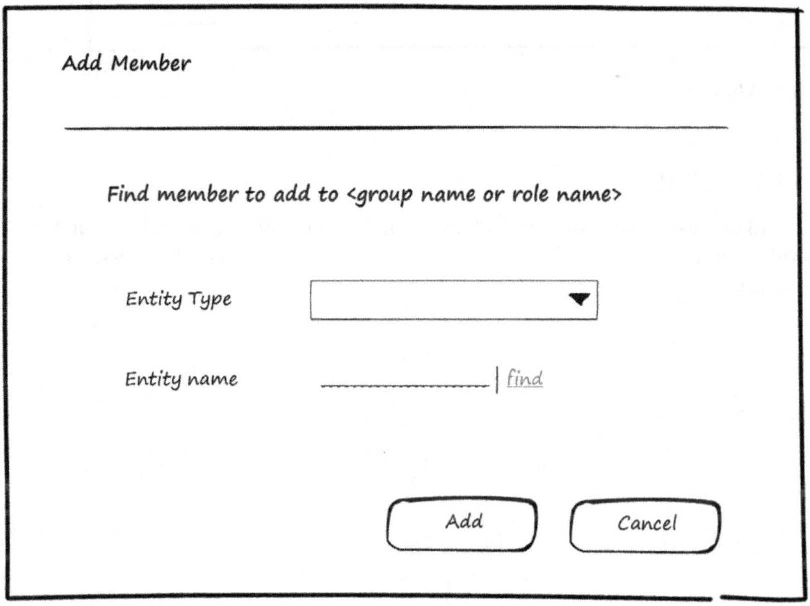

Figure 8-11. *Find entity to add to a group*

Entity type can be selected and then searching is enabled for the entity of that type to be added as a member. Types of entities that can be added are User, Role, Position, Position Type, and Organization.

Roles Page

This page is used to manage roles. Users can search, view, add, edit, and delete roles in the system. Figure 8-12 shows a wireframe for listing roles.

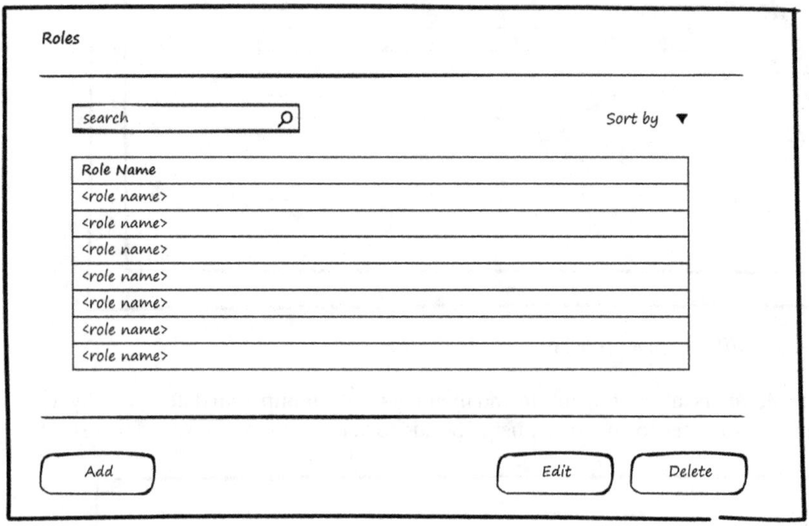

Figure 8-12. Manage roles

Role Editor Page

In Figures 8-13 and 8-14, you can see wireframes for the Role Editor page, which can be used for editing or adding roles. This page has two tabs: Basic Info and Members, for members (players) of the role.

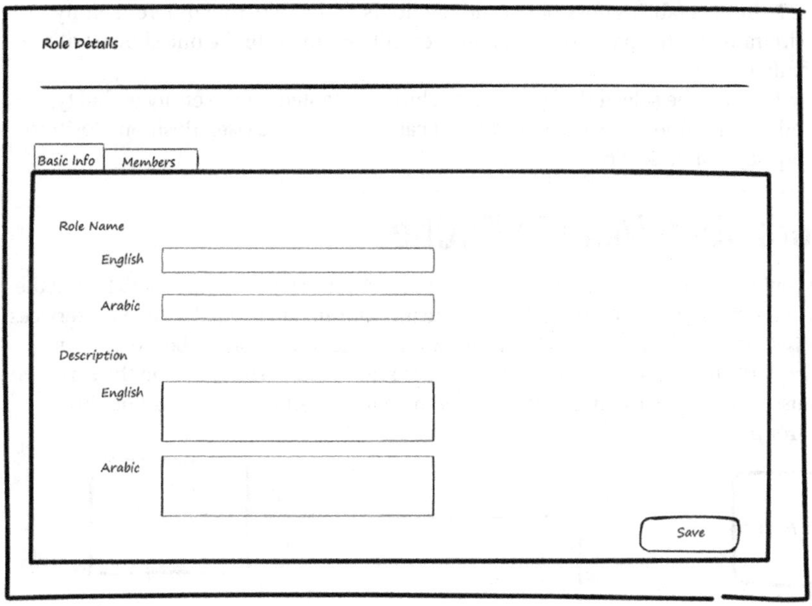

Figure 8-13. *Edit role: basic info*

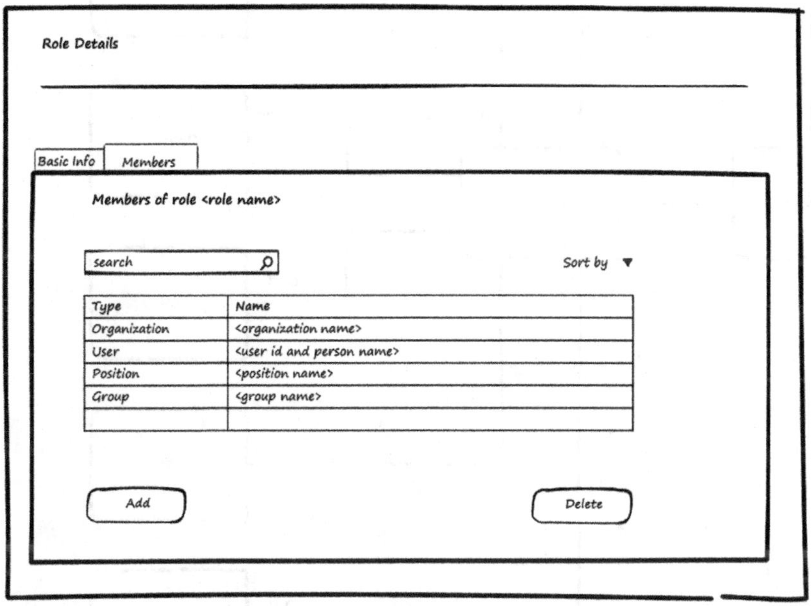

Figure 8-14. *Edit role: members*

In the Members tab, it's possible to add members to the role from different entity types. A wireframe for the page to find a member will be similar to the one shown with a group member.

Entity Type can be selected and then searching is enabled for the entity of that type to be added as a member. Types of entities that can be added are User, Position, Position Type, Group, and Organization.

Authorization Module Entities

Now that you've seen use-cases and wireframes for the Authorization module, let's look at the entities used by the Authorization module to store the information needed to manage services and permissions. Figures 8-15 through 8-17 show the entities and relations between them.

Figure 8-15 shows the entities used to store services and permissions on the services. The permission on service can be given to Organization, Position Type, Position, Role, User, or Group.

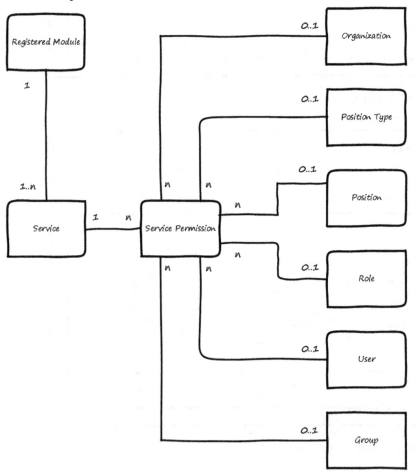

Figure 8-15. *Entities for the Authorization module: services and permission*

104

Figure 8-16 shows the entities used to store members of groups. The group member can be Organization, Position Type, Position, Role, or User.

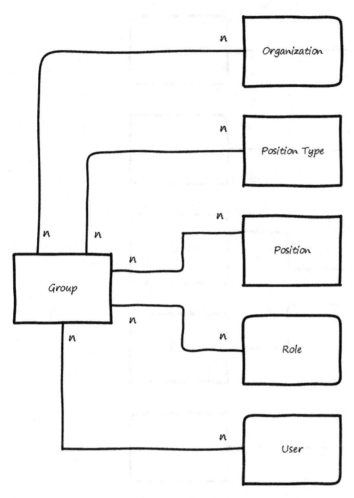

Figure 8-16. *Entities for the Authorization module: group members*

Figure 8-17 shows the entities used to store members of roles. The role member can be Organization, Position Type, Position, Group, or User.

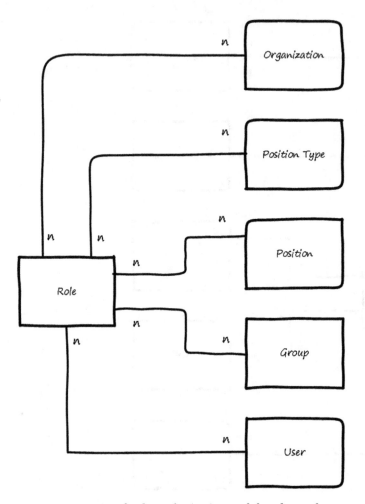

***Figure 8-17.** Entities for the Authorization module: role members*

Here are descriptions of the entities appearing in Figures 8-15 through 8-17:

- *Registered Module*: Stores data about the modules that registered themselves to be managed by the Authorization module.

- *Group*: Stores basic information about the groups and its members.

- *Role*: Stores basic information about the role and its member (players).

- *Service*: Stores basic information about the services.

- *Service Permission*: Stores permissions given to entities on the services.

The relations between these entities can be summarized as follows:

- Registered Module can provide multiple services.

- Service can have multiple permissions given on them.

- Organization, Position Type, Position, Role, User, and Group can have permission on multiple services.

- Group can have multiple members of types: Organization, Position Type, Position, Role, and User.

- Organization, Position Type, Position, Role, and User can be a member of multiple groups.

- Role can have multiple members (players) of types Organization, Position Type, Position, Group, and User.

- Organization, Position Type, Position, Group, and User can be a member of (players with assigned) multiple roles.

Use of the Authorization Module by Other Modules

The Authorization module accepts other modules to be plugged into it so that the services for other modules can be managed by the Authorization module.

Modules can be plugged into the Authorization module using the register module use-case. In order to be registered, they should implement the register module interface. The interface will need the module (to be registered) to be able to answer the following questions, and the answer will be used to fill the entities as described:

- *Who are you?* The answer to this question will be saved in the Registered Module entity.

- *What services do you provide?* Answer will be saved in Service entity.

- *What groups do you use?* Answer will be saved in the Group entity.

- *What roles do you use?* Answer will be saved in the Role entity.

After a module is plugged into the Authorization module, it will be able to use the Is user authorized use-case, the Get user authorized services use-case, and the other use-cases provided by the Authorization module to the registered module.

Summary

This chapter discussed the Authorization module, including what authorization is and why it's required. I discussed the use-cases for Authorization module and showed wireframes for the screens. You were introduced to the entities and their relations. In the last section, you saw how other modules could use the Authorization module.

CHAPTER 9

■ ■ ■

Communication Rules Module

Persons who use a software system need to communicate, which means every software system should be flexible in defining and managing the communication among its users. The system administrator should be able to define the rules for communication. The Communication Rules module's main functionality is to enable software systems to manage the definition of rules that control how users communicate together and evaluate these rules to ensure that every person can communicate with persons without violating the communication rules.

After finishing this chapter, you will be able to answer the following questions:

- What are communication rules?

- Why do you need communication rules?

- How should you store communication rules' data?

- What does the UI for the Communication rules module look like?

A *communication rule* defines who can communicate with whom inside the system. *Communication* is the process of sending messages or asking for something from a sender (*source*) to a receiver (*destination*). By defining communication rules in the system, we can control who can communicate with whom.

The Communication Rule has a source and a destination, plus communication options.

- *Source*: This is the first part in communication. It represents the sender of the communication message. A source can be Level, Organization, Position, Position Type, Role, Person, or Group. For Level, Organization, and Group it's possible to select items from inside these entities. For example, if the source is a group, you can specify whether the source is all the members of the group or a subset of the members.

© Mohamed Farouk 2017
M. Farouk, *Infrastructure Software Modules for Enterprises*,
DOI 10.1007/978-1-4842-3021-3_9

- *Destination*: This is the second part of communication.
  It represents the receiver of the communication message.
  Destination can be Level, Organization, Position, Position Type,
  Role, Person, or Group. For Level, Organization, and Group it's
  possible to select items from inside these entities.

- *Options*: There are two options for each communication rule.
  The first option is communication type, which can be *allow*
  or *deny*. Allow means the source can communication with the
  destination, and deny means the source cannot communicate
  with the destination. The second option is communication
  direction, which can be *one way* or *two way*. One way means that
  communication rule applies from source to destination, and two
  way means the rule is applied in both direction. For example,
  if Communication Rule has the options allow and one way, it
  means the source is allowed to communicate with the destination
  but the destination cannot communicate with the source. If the
  options are allow and two way, it means the source is allowed to
  communicate with the destination and the destination is allowed
  to communicate with the source.

After communication rules are defined, when communication operation is
requested in the system the system will send the person who wants to communicate
to the Communication Rules module. Then the Communication Rules module will
evaluate the communication rules and return a list with persons that are allowed as the
communication destination.

Importance of Communication Rules

We need communication rules to control who can communicate with whom. For
example, sending a message to another person. If you are allowed to communicate
with that person, you will be able to send the message to them directly. In addition,
communication is useful in assigning tasks to another person. If you are allowed to
communicate with a person, you will be able to create and assign tasks for them. The
communication rules are declared based on the organization policy. If the organization
wants to control the communication or to make it open, that can be done from the
Communication Rules module.

Communication Rules Module Use-Cases

Figure 9-1 shows use-cases for Communication Rules module. Actors for these use-
cases are the user who has permission to manage the rules and the system module,
which can be a business module or infrastructure module that needs to get the allowed
communication list for a user.

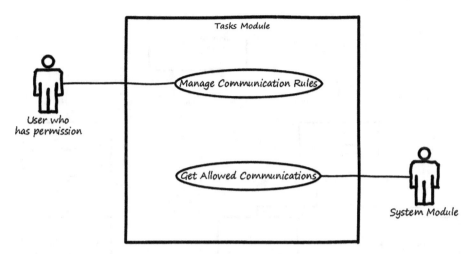

Figure 9-1. *Use-cases for the Communication Rules module*

Here is a description for each use-case:

- *Manage communication rules*: This use-case is used to enable the user to search, view, add, modify, and test communication rules.

- *Get allowed communications*: This use-case is used to enable the other modules to receive a list of allowed communication destinations for a specific person.

Communication Rules Module Wireframes

This section shows high-level wireframe screens for the Communication Rules module. The UI flow is shown in Figure 9-2.

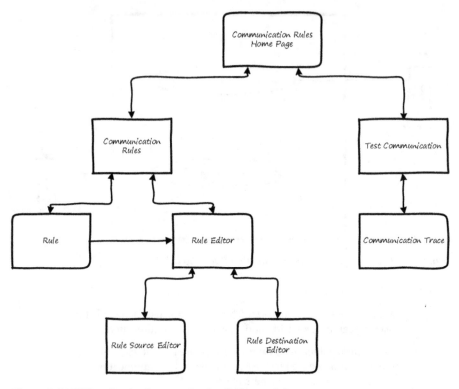

Figure 9-2. *UI flow for the Communication Rules module*

From the home page, a user can manage the communication rules by navigating to the Communication Rules page. On this page, the user can search, add, view, edit, and delete communication rules. To view the rule, the user will navigate to the Rule page, and to edit or create a rule, they will navigate to the Rule Editor page. From there, the user will be able to edit the source and destination of the rule by navigating to pages called Rule Source Editor and Rule Destination Editor. To test a communication, the user can go from the home page to the Test Communication page, and they can trace the communication result by navigating to the Communication Trace page.

Communication Rules Page

The Communication Rules page displays all defined communication rules. The user can search, add, edit, or delete rules.

Figure 9-3 shows a wireframe screen for listing communication rules.

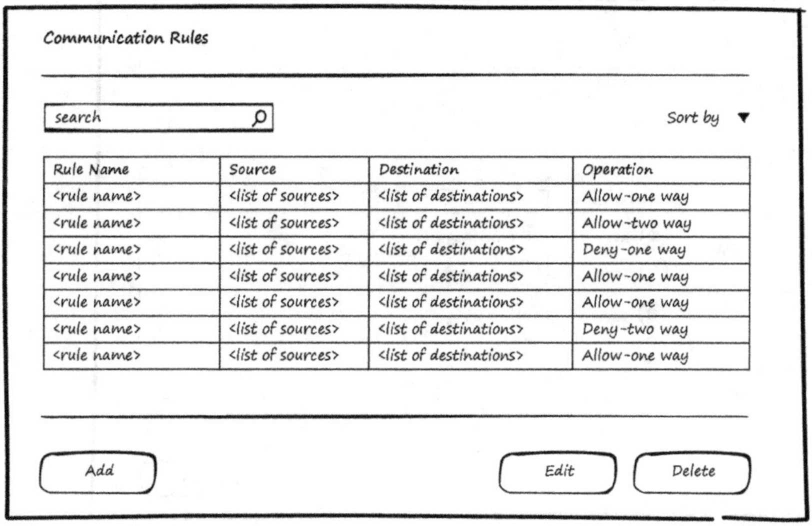

Communication Rules

Rule Name	Source	Destination	Operation
<rule name>	<list of sources>	<list of destinations>	Allow–one way
<rule name>	<list of sources>	<list of destinations>	Allow–two way
<rule name>	<list of sources>	<list of destinations>	Deny–one way
<rule name>	<list of sources>	<list of destinations>	Allow–one way
<rule name>	<list of sources>	<list of destinations>	Allow–one way
<rule name>	<list of sources>	<list of destinations>	Deny–two way
<rule name>	<list of sources>	<list of destinations>	Allow–one way

Figure 9-3. *List communication rules*

Communication Rule Editor Page

In Figure 9-4, you can see the wireframe for the Communication Rule page in edit mode, which can be used for editing or adding a rule. A rule has a name and items, and each communication item consists of a source, operation (communication and direction), and destination.

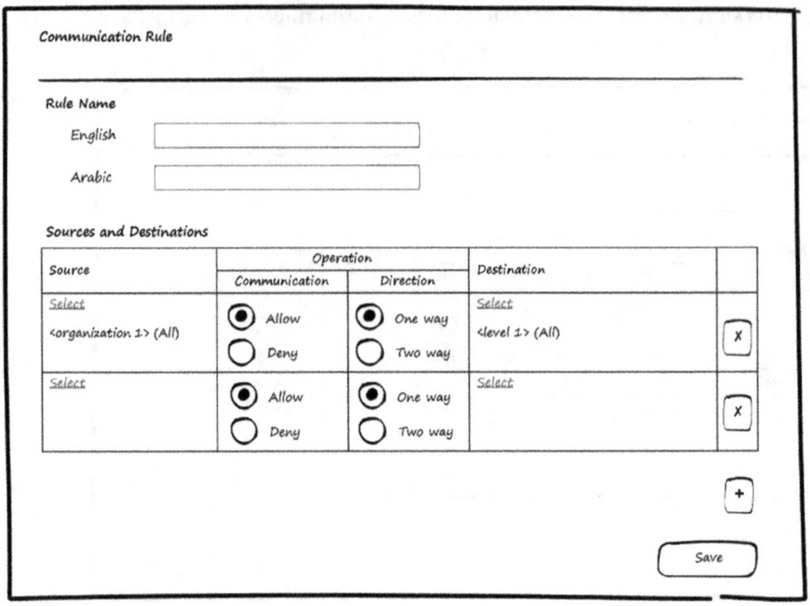

Figure 9-4. *Edit communication rules*

The Communication Rules page depends on the Localization module to support entering a rule's name in the supported languages.

Rule Source Page

From the Communication Rule Editor page, the user can Click the Select link in the Source column for a rule's item. The system then opens the Source page. Figure 9-5 shows a wireframe for the Source page in edit mode. The user can select the source type, which can be Level, Organization, Position Type, Position, Role, Group, or Person, and then select the name for the selected type. If the selected entity name contains inner members, the system displays a list of this members and allows the user to select all or select specific items from the list. It's also possible to filter the inner members by type. In Figure 9-5, you see an exsample of selecting type Level. The Level type refers to the levels of the organization structure. Therefore, in this case, the source name will contain Level 1, Level 2, and so on, based on the number of levels in the organization structure. The level's inner members will be the organizations in this level, the position types and positions in this level, and the persons working in the positions in this level.

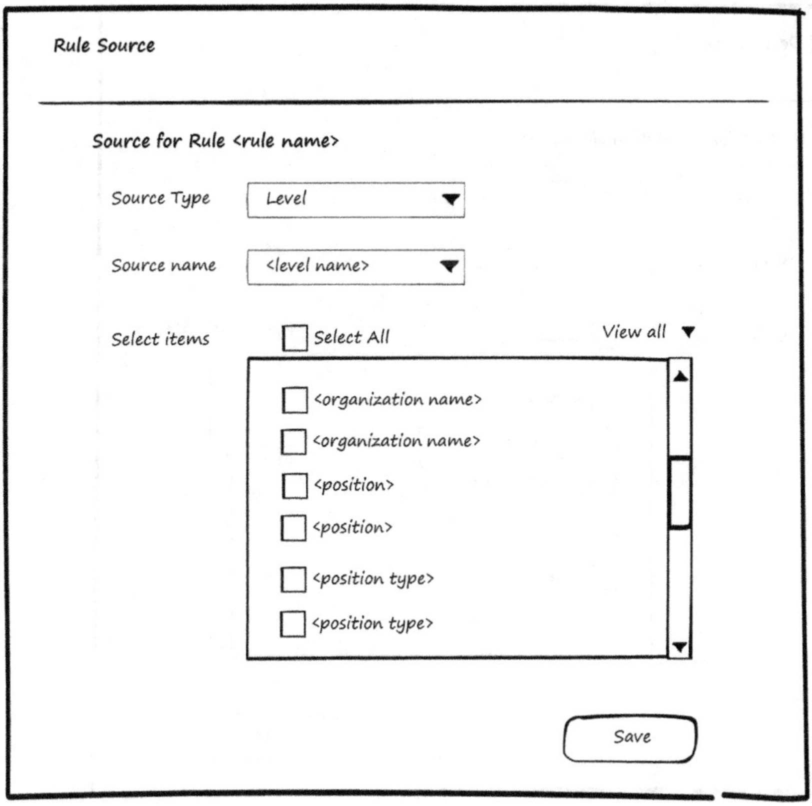

Figure 9-5. *Edit rule source*

Rule Destination Page

From the Communication Rule editor page, the user can click the Select link in the Destination column for a rule's item, and the system will opens the Destination page. Figure 9-6 shows a wireframe for the Destination page in edit mode, which is similar to the Source page described in the previous section.

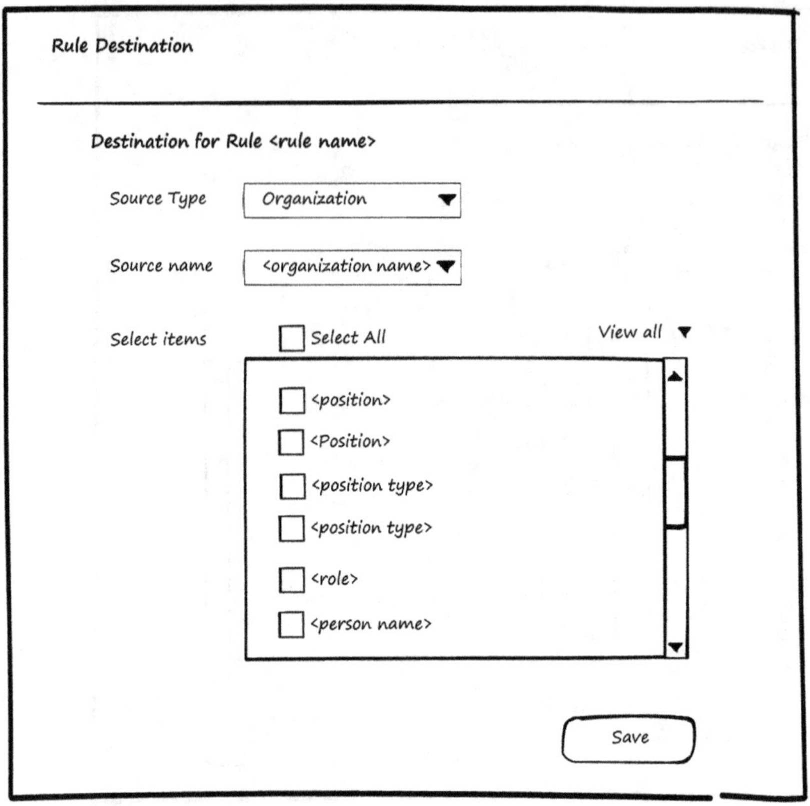

Rule Destination

Destination for Rule <rule name>

Source Type   [Organization ▼]

Source name   [<organization name> ▼]

Select items   ☐ Select All   View all ▼

☐ <position>
☐ <Position>
☐ <position type>
☐ <position type>
☐ <role>
☐ <person name>

(Save)

Figure 9-6. *Edit rule destination*

In Figure 9-6, you can see an example of selecting type Organization. In this case, the destination name will contain the names of the organizations defined in the system. The organization inner members will be the position types and positions in this organization, the persons working in this organization, and the roles of position types and positions in this organization.

Test Communication Page

Figure 9-7 shows a wireframe for the Test Communication page. Here, a user can enter the name of a person or position, and then the system will display list of positions (and the persons work in these positions) that can communicate with them. The communication can be allowed or denied. To see why the communication is allowed or denied, the user can click the Trace link to open the Communication Trace page.

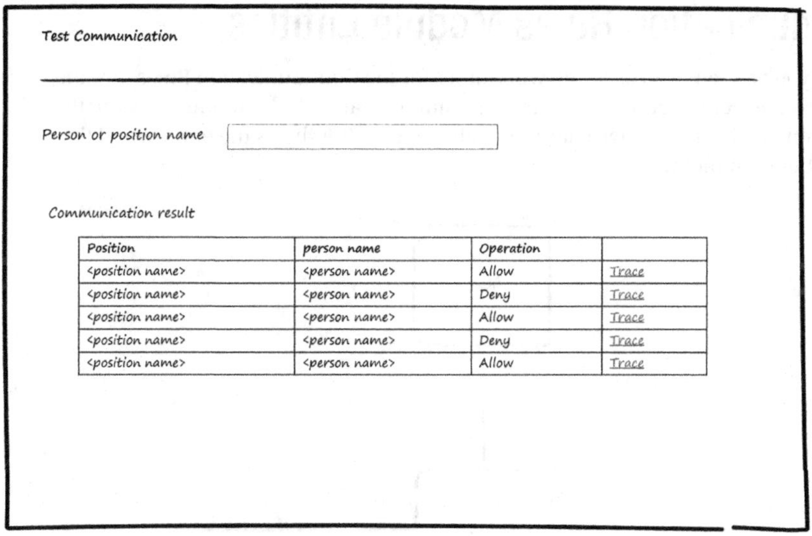

Test Communication

Person or position name

Communication result

Position	person name	Operation	
<position name>	<person name>	Allow	Trace
<position name>	<person name>	Deny	Trace
<position name>	<person name>	Allow	Trace
<position name>	<person name>	Deny	Trace
<position name>	<person name>	Allow	Trace

Figure 9-7. *Test communication*

Communication Trace Page

This page is used to display the rules that are applied to get the communication result (allow or deny). Figure 9-8 shows a wireframe for the Communication Trace page.

Communication Trace

Source   <Position name> – <person name>

Destination <Position name> – <person name>

Applied rules

Rule	Result
<rule name>	Allow
<rule name>	Deny
<rule name>	Allow
<rule name>	Deny
<rule name>	Allow

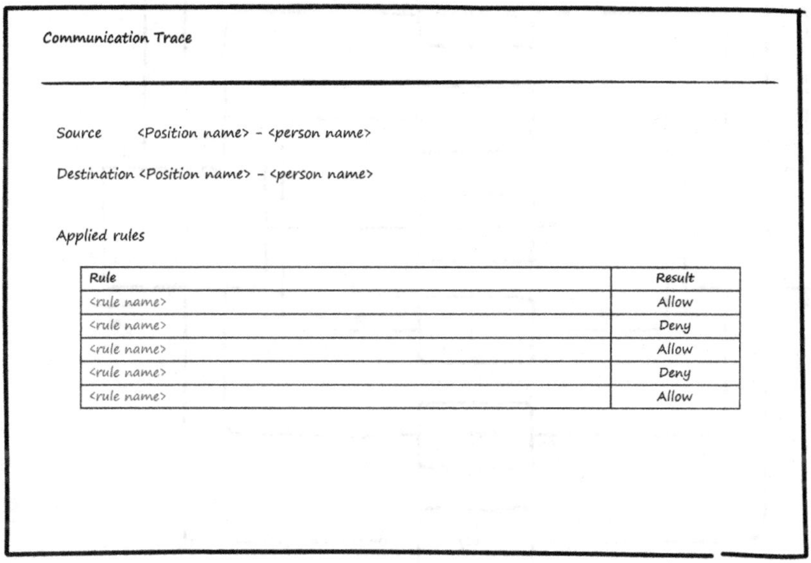

Figure 9-8. *Trace communication*

Communication Rules Module Entities

Now that you've seen use-cases and wireframes for the Communication Rules module, it's time to consider the entities used by the Communication Rules module to store the information needed to manage communication. Figure 9-9 shows the entities and the relations between them.

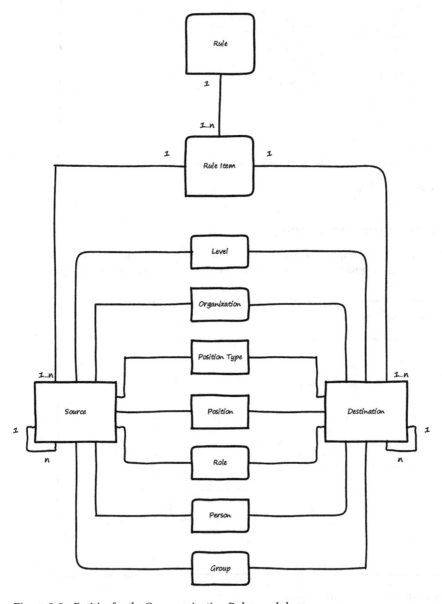

Figure 9-9. *Entities for the Communication Rules module*

Here is a description for each entity:

- *Rule*: Stores the Name of the rule.

- *Rule Item*: Stores the main data of the rule's item (Name, Communication Type, Communication Direction, Source, Destination).

- *Source*: Stores the source data for the Communication Rule's item.

- *Destination*: Stores the destination data for the Communication Rule's item.

The relations between these entities can be summarized as follows:

- Rule must have at least one Rule Item.

- Rule Item must have at least one Source and one Destination.

- Rule Item can have multiple Sources and multiple Destinations.

- Source or Destination can be any of the following: Level, Organization, Position Type, Position, Role, Person, or Group.

- If the Source or Destination is an entity that contains items (such as Level, Organization, Organization, or Group), then the Source or the Destination may have sub-sources and sub-destinations in order to fine-tune the Communication Rule.

Use of the Communication Rules Module by Other Modules

No modules need to register to use the Communication Rules module. Other modules can directly use the get allowed communication use-case.

Summary

This chapter discussed the Communication Rules module, including what communication rules are and why you need them. Use-cases and wireframes for the screens were shown, and you saw the entities used to store the communication rules and their relations.

CHAPTER 10

■ ■ ■

Tasks Module

To complete an operation or a process in a software system, tasks need to be assigned and performed. Some tasks are assigned to users or the system, and some tasks can be performed automatically by the system. Persons who have tasks assigned to them need to be able to manage these tasks. This means every software system should provide a mechanism to handle tasks. The Tasks module's main functionality is to enable software systems to manage tasks assigned to persons, allowing the persons to perform, delegate, and track the tasks.

After finishing this chapter, you will be able to answer the following questions:

- What are tasks and types of tasks are there?

- What is the relation between communication rules and tasks?

- How should you store tasks data?

- What does the UI for the Tasks module look like?

A *task* is something to be done. This thing to be done can be done by persons (users of the system) either manually outside the system or inside the system by using the functionality supported in the system based on the nature of the task.

A task that can be performed manually will have a description, but a task that can be performed inside the system will have a form and action buttons to be performed.

The following are possible types of tasks:

- *Normal*: A manual task that has only description about it.

- *Payment*: A task that displays an invoice and can be performed by paying money. Payment can be done by different methods (see Chapter 14).

- *Inspection*: A task that displays an inspection form to be filled by person.

- *Review*: A task that displays something and asks the user to enter comments on it.

- *Decision*: A task that displays something and asks the user to approve or reject it.

- *Custom*: A task that display a custom form and can perform custom actions.

© Mohamed Farouk 2017
M. Farouk, *Infrastructure Software Modules for Enterprises*,
DOI 10.1007/978-1-4842-3021-3_10

Normal tasks can be assembled as a project. Other task types in most cases will be part of the workflow (business process—see Chapter 11).

Communication rules control how tasks can be assigned or delegated. A task can be created by a person and assigned to the same person or another person. Every person who creates a task can assign it to a person with whom they can communicate, based on the communication rules defined in the Communication Rules module.

If a task is assigned to a person, they can delegate it to another person. To delegate, the user selects a person with whom they can communicate (based on the communication rules).

Tasks Module Use-Cases

Figure 10-1 shows use-cases for the Tasks module. Actors for these use-cases are any user to manage his own tasks, a user who has permission to manage all tasks, and a system module, which is either a business module or infrastructure module that registers the tasks.

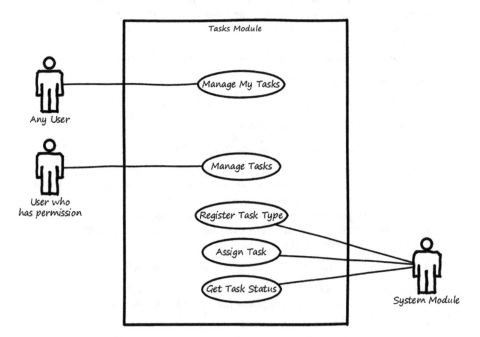

Figure 10-1. *Use-cases for the Tasks module*

Here is a description for each use-case:

- *Manage my tasks*: This use-case is used to enable the user to search, view, add, modify, perform, delegate, and delete tasks assigned to them or created by them.

- *Manage tasks*: This use-case is used to enable the user to search, view, modify, reassign, and delete any task.

- *Register task type*: This use-case is used to enable other modules to add new a task type and to register the Task Editor page and the Task Performer page that will be used with the new type.

- *Assign Task*: This use-case is used to enable other modules to assign tasks to be performed by users in the system.

- *Get Tasks Status*: This use-case is used to inform its actor about the status of a certain task.

Tasks Module Wireframes

This section shows high-level wireframe screens for the Tasks module. The UI flow is shown in Figure 10-2.

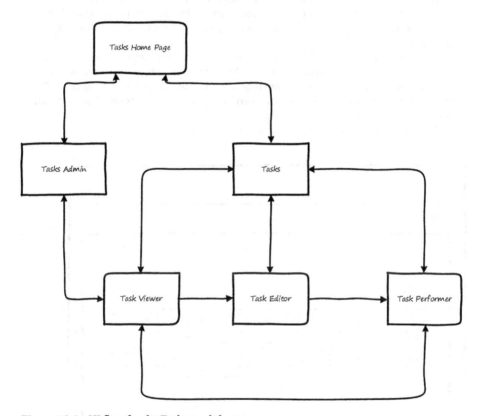

Figure 10-2. *UI flow for the Tasks module*

From the home page of the Tasks module, the user can navigate to the Tasks page where they can view tasks assigned to or created by them and search and manage the tasks. The user can navigate to the Tasks Editor page to create or modify a task, and to view a task the user can select a task and navigate to the Task Viewer page. The Task Viewer

123

page enables the user to see the task information, history, and performing data. From the Viewer page, the user can also go to the Editor page to edit the task. To perform the task, the user needs to navigate to the Task Performer page where they can complete the task.

For administration purposes, the admin user can navigate to the Task Admin page. The Task Admin page views all tasks created or assigned to any user. From this page, the admin user can view, modify, delete, or reassign tasks.

In the rest of this section, we will see what these pages look like.

Tasks Page

When a user creates a task or a task is assigned to them, these tasks will appear in the Tasks page. From this page, the user will be able to manage the tasks. The page will display the tasks assigned to the current user in the Tasks tab. Tasks delegated (reassigned) by the user to other users will be displayed in the Delegated tab.

The user can create tasks or edit tasks they created. In addition, the user can delete tasks they created. For tasks assigned to them, they can perform the task or delegate it to another user.

A task can be assigned or delegated to different types of entities (Person, Position, Position Type, Group, Organization, or Role). When a task is assigned to an entity that represents multiple persons (Group, Organization, Role, or Position Type), the task will be put in a queue. This queue will be displayed to the users who represent this entity, and a user can pick the task from the queue and perform it.

Figure 10-3 shows a wireframe for listing tasks.

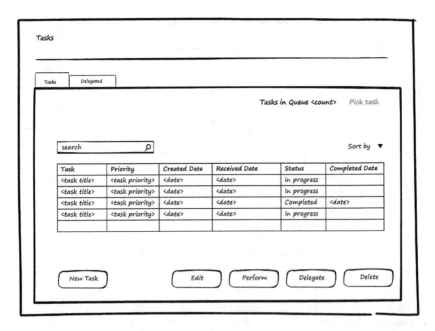

Figure 10-3. *Manage tasks*

There are two tabs in the tasks page. The Tasks tab is for the tasks assigned to the user, and the Delegated tab displays the tasks delegated by the user to other users.

As shown in Figure 10-4, the page displays the delegated tasks and to whom they are assigned and their status. From this page, the user can cancel the delegation of a task (if it's not completed yet), and it will appear in the Tasks tab.

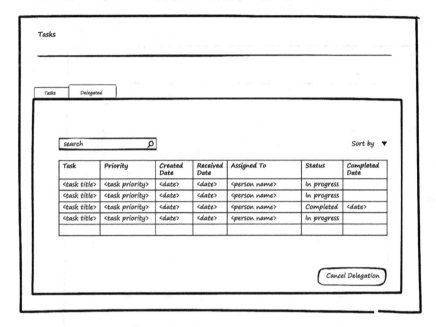

Figure 10-4. *Manage delegated tasks*

Task Editor Page

In Figure 10-5, you can see the wireframe for the Task Editor page, which can be used for editing or adding task. Each task has a type, and the Task module uses Normal type. However, other modules can register other types of tasks. The Normal task type has a Description field. Other task types will register their UI element to be used instead of the description.

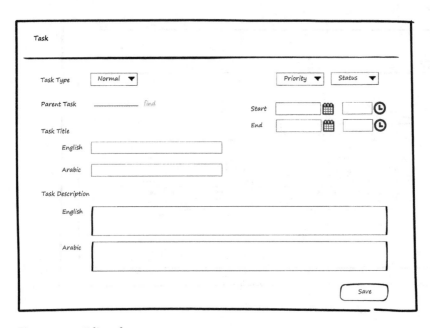

Figure 10-5. *Edit task*

A task can be a subtask of another task, so there is an option to select a parent task.

The Task Editor page depends on the Localization module to support entering task names and descriptions in the supported languages.

Task Delegation Page

By default, a created task is assigned to its creator. A user can assign a task to another user by selecting a task and clicking the Delegate button (on the Tasks page—refer to Figure 10-3).

Figure 10-6 shows the Delegation page. Here, the user can assign a task to an entity (the entity could be Position, Position Type, Group, Organization, Role, or Person) by clicking the Find link, which will open a page to allow the user to search for the entity to assign a task for it.

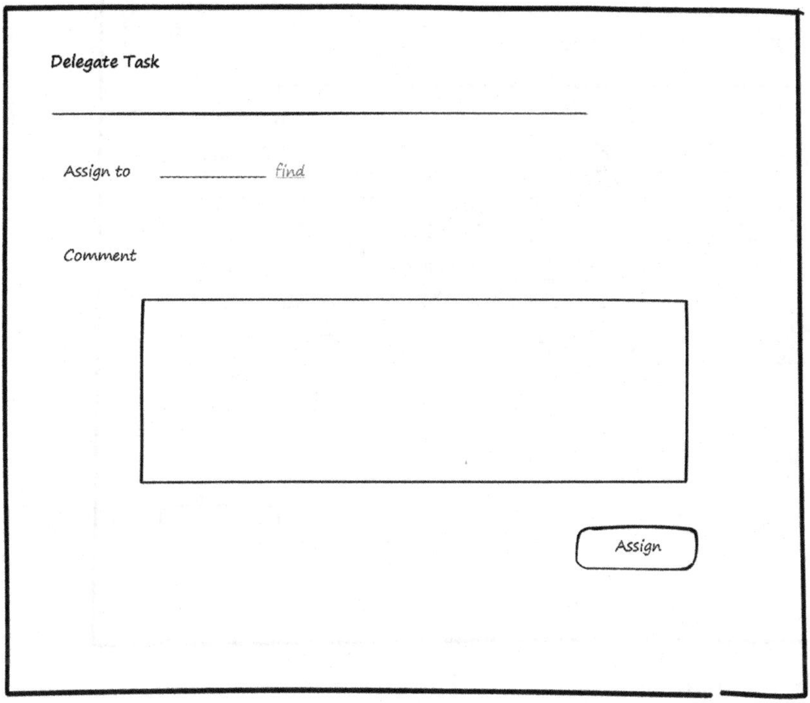

Figure 10-6. *Delegate task*

*The u*ser can enter a comment, and the task will be assigned. As mentioned, if a task is assigned to an entity that represents multiple persons (Position Type, Group, Organization, or Role), the task will be placed in the Task Queue, where it can be picked by any user who belongs to the entity.

Task Queue Page

The Task Queue page can be opened from the Tasks page when the user clicks the Pick Task link. The Task Queue displays the tasks assigned to entities that the user belongs to (Position Type, Role, Organization, or Group). Figure 10-7 shows the Task Queue page where the user can search for and pick tasks. Picked tasks will be assigned to the user and removed from the queue. They will appear in the Tasks page and be shown as tasks assigned to the user.

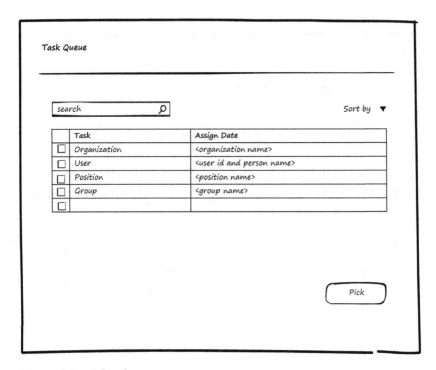

Figure 10-7. Pick task

Task Performer Page

This page will differ based on the task type. For the Normal tasks supported by the Tasks module, it will be like the wireframe shown in Figure 10-8. For other task types, the system will show the UI element associated with the task type, which was registered by the module that owns the task type.

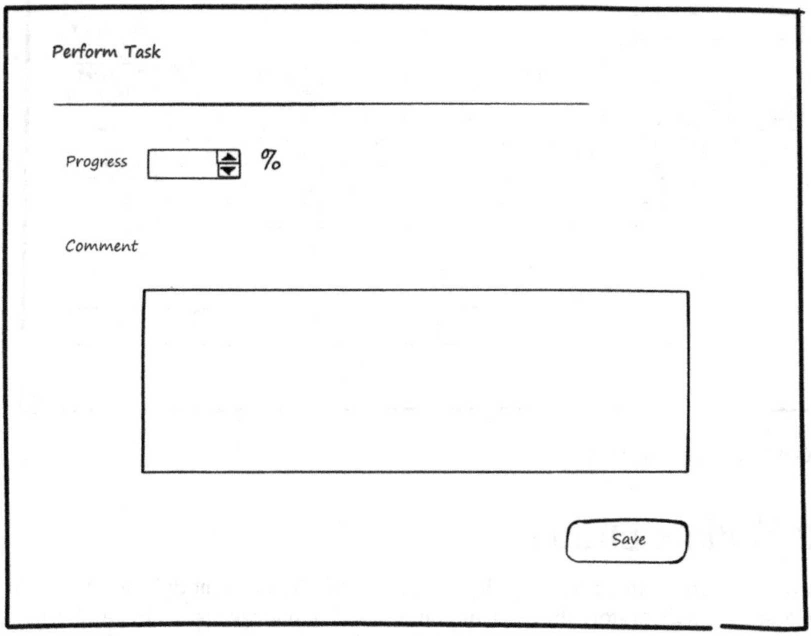

Figure 10-8. *Perform task*

Tasks Admin Page

The system administrator or the user who has permission to be the tasks admin can use this page to search for tasks assigned to any user or created by any user and manage them. The admin can view, edit, perform, reassign, or delete tasks.

Figure 10-9 shows a wireframe for listing tasks.

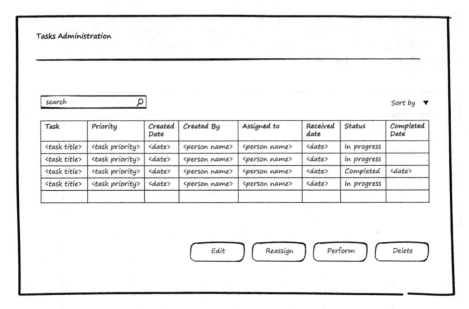

Figure 10-9. *Manage tasks: admin*

Tasks Module Entities

Now that you've seen the use-cases and the wireframes for the Tasks module, it's time to see the entities it uses to store the information needed to manage tasks. Figure 10-10 shows the entities and relations between them.

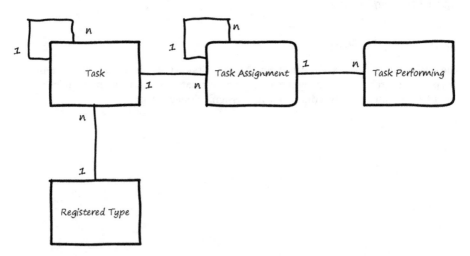

Figure 10-10. *Entities for the Tasks module*

Here is a description for each entity:

- *Registered Type*: Stores information about the type and the UI elements that will be used to edit the task data and perform the task.

- *Task*: Stores the type and data for the task.

- *Task Assignment*: Stores the task assignment to an entity (Person, Group, Organization, Position, Position Type, or Role).

- *Task Performing*: Stores the main performing data for tasks. If the type of the task is other than Normal, more entities will be used to store the performing data based on the type and the module that uses this type.

The relations between these entities can be summarized as follows:

- Task can have multiple subtasks.

- Task may have one parent or it may be without a parent if it's not a subtask.

- Task can have multiple assignments (can be reassigned many times, but it has only one active assignment).

- Task Assignment can reference another Task Assignment (to know whom to delegate the assignment to).

- Task Assignment can be performed gradually (progress can be updated multiple times).

Use of the Tasks Module by Other Modules

The Tasks module accepts other modules to be plugged into it in order to enable new task types to be used.

Modules can be plugged into the Tasks module using the register task type use-case. In order to be registered, they should implement the Register Task Type interface. The interface will need the module (to be registered) to be able to answer the following questions, and the answer will be used to fill the entities as described:

- *What type do you want to register?* The answer to this question will be saved in the Registered Types entity.

- *What is the UI element to edit the task?* The answer will be saved in the Registered Types entity.

- *What is the UI element to perform the task?* The answer will be saved in the Registered Types entity.

After a task type is plugged into the Tasks module, the module that requested the registration can use the assign task use-case to assign tasks of the new type to users and the get task status use-case to inquire about the task's status.

Summary

This chapter discussed the Tasks module, including what tasks are, their types, and the relationship between communication rules and tasks. I discussed use-cases for the Tasks module and showed wireframes for the screens. You were introduced to the entities and their relations, and in the last section, you saw how other modules could use the Tasks module.

■ ■ ■

CHAPTER 11

Workflow Module

Every organization has a set of defined business activities, or *processes*. Examples might include requests to be reviewed and either approved or rejected. Other examples would include complex processes to be completed by going through steps where, in every step, one or more tasks need to be performed either by a person or by the system. We call such a process and its steps a *workflow*. The software system should be flexible in defining workflows, their steps, and who performs them. The Workflow module's main functionality is to enable software systems to manage workflow definitions and instances.

After finishing this chapter, you will be able to answer the following questions:

- What are workflows and how do they relate to tasks?

- What are common types of tasks used with workflows?

- What are workflow instances?

- How should you store workflow definitions and instances?

- How does the UI for the Workflow module look?

A workflow is a sequence of industrial, administrative, or other processes through which a piece of work passes from initiation to completion. The path from initiation to completion is a set of steps, and every step corresponds to a task. This task may be human task that needs to be performed by a user or a system task that can be performed by the system.

A workflow *definition* defines the steps that the workflow will go through and the conditions to go from step to another. In addition, the workflow definition defines the data that is required for the workflow. When a workflow is initiated, it's called an *instance*. Each instance will have its own data and go through its own route.

As mentioned, tasks can be categorized into user tasks and system tasks. User tasks are tasks assigned to a user to be performed. Here are some examples of user tasks:

- *Review task*: A user reviews some data and enters notes on it.

- *Decision task*: A user makes a decision to approve or reject the workflow instance.

- *Inspection task*: A user fills out an inspection form related to the workflow instance.

© Mohamed Farouk 2017
M. Farouk, *Infrastructure Software Modules for Enterprises*,
DOI 10.1007/978-1-4842-3021-3_11

- *Payment task*: A user pays or collects fees for the workflow instance.

- *Sign task*: A user digitally or electronically signs an application related to the workflow instance.

- *Custom task*: A user performs a custom action defined by the module that owns the workflow.

System tasks are tasks assigned to the system and performed by the system. Here are some examples of system tasks:

- *Notification task*: The system sends a notification to users or systems related to the workflow instance.

- *Integration task*: The system calls an API from another system to provide it with data related to the workflow instance.

- *Action task*: The system performs an internal action (calling an API in the system to do something).

- *Waiting task*: The system waits for a period or until some dependent task is completed.

- *Transition task*: The system evaluates a condition and then routes the workflow to a certain step based on the condition.

- *Escalation task*: The system reassigns a task to a certain user if no progress is made on the task for a certain period of time.

User tasks can have the following attributes, which can be configured in the task definition for the workflow. A user task

- Can send notification.

- Can ask for consultation.

- Can return to the previous task.

- Can request attachments or data modification from the initiator.

- Can reassign the task.

- Can create subtasks.

- Can be assigned to multiple users.

Workflow Module Use-Cases

Figure 11-1 shows use-cases for the Workflow module. Actors for these use-cases are the user who has permission to manage workflow definitions and the system module, which can be a business module or infrastructure module that needs to register its workflow definitions.

134

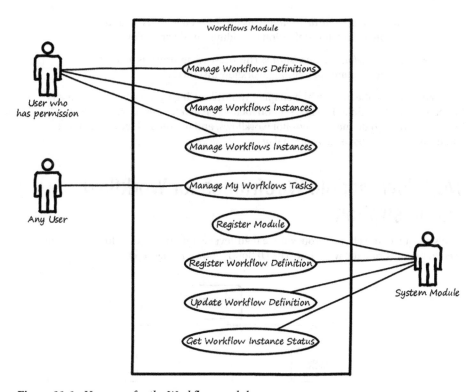

Figure 11-1. *Use-cases for the Workflow module*

The workflow module is responsible for providing the mechanism to define the workflows and to operate the workflow's instances.

Here is a description for each use-case:

- *Manage workflow definition*: This use-case enables the user to search, view, add, modify, delete, publish, and unpublish workflow definitions.

- *Manage my workflow instances*: This use-case enables the user to search, initiate, view, and cancel workflow instances they created.

- *Manage workflow instances*: This use-case enables the user to search, view, reassign, and terminate workflow instances.

- *Register module*: This use-case enables another module to register itself and the definitions of workflow it uses to be managed by the Workflow module. Task types used by these workflow definitions will be registered in the Tasks module.

- *Register workflow definition*: This use-case enables its actor to register a new workflow definition to be managed by the Workflow module.

135

- *Update workflow definition*: This use-case enables its actor to update a workflow definition by adding a new version of it.

- *Get workflow instance status*: This use-case informs its actor about the status of a certain workflow instance.

In the next two sections of the chapter, you will see high-level wireframe screens for the Workflow module. The first section focuses on wireframes of screens used by administrator to define and monitor workflows, and the second section explores wireframes for screens used by normal users.

Workflow Module Wireframes for Workflow Administration

In this section of the chapter, you will see high-level wireframe screens for the screens used to administrate the workflow. The UI flow is shown in Figure 11-2.

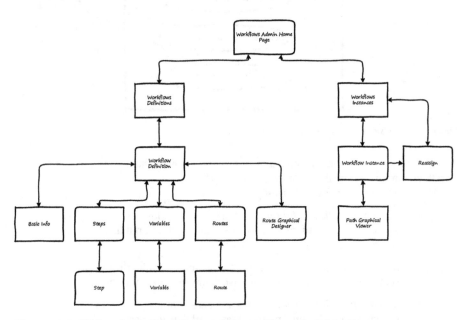

Figure 11-2. *UI flow for the Workflow module: workflow administration*

From the home page of the Workflow module, the user can navigate either to workflow definitions or to workflow instances. The Workflow Definitions page enables the user to view the existing workflow definitions and manage them by searching, viewing, adding, or modifying. The user can select a definition to modify or can select to add a new definition. In this case, the system navigates the user to the Workflow Definition page, which consist of four sub-pages to handle the workflow definition. The user can define the workflow by setting the basic information from the Basic Info page and defining the steps by navigating to the Steps page that lists the defined steps. The step information can be managed from the Step page. Variables used in the workflow can be found in the Variables page, which lets the user manage the variables. Variable information can be defined on the Variable page. The user can also define the routes between the steps from the Routes page. In addition, a graphical designer for the workflow can be used. The Route Graphical Designer page is used for graphically defining the routes.

After the workflow is defined (or registered by other modules), instances will be crated. The admin can monitor these instances by navigating from the home page to the Workflow Instances page, which enables the user to search the existing instances of the workflow. To view the workflow instance's data, the user goes to the Workflow Instance page. From there, if the workflow instance is active and has a task assigned to a certain user, the admin user can choose to reassign this task to another user from the Reassign page. The user can view the exact path that the workflow instance goes through from the Path Graphical Viewer page.

The rest of this section shows wireframes for some of these pages.

Workflow Definitions Page

When modules register themselves and their workflows in the Workflow module, their workflows definitions will appear in the Workflow Definitions page.

This page allows the administrator user to search, view, and modify existing workflow definitions. The user can also create a new version of a workflow definition, which can be published after it has been defined.

When users request to initiate new workflow instance, the Workflow module will initiate it from the latest version. The currently active workflow instances will use the version that they were created from.

Figure 11-3 shows a wireframe for listing workflow definitions.

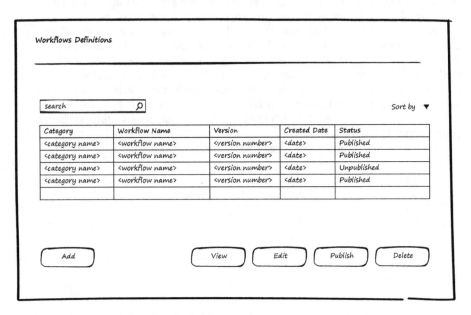

Figure 11-3. Manage Workflow Definitions

Workflow Definition Page

In Figure 11-4, you can see a wireframe for the Workflow Definition page in edit mode, which can be used for modifying a definition or creating a new version. The Workflow Definition page contains five tabs.

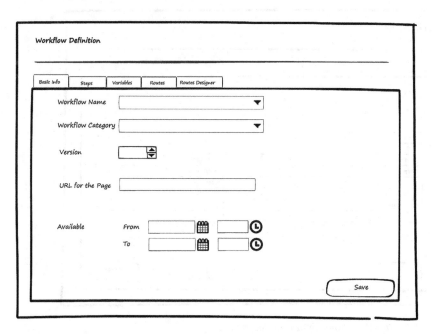

Figure 11-4. *Edit Workflow Definition: Basic Info tab*

Basic Info

The first tab is Basic Info (shown in Figure 11-4), where the user can select a workflow and set the version. An important field is the URL for the Page, which will handle this workflow. In our Workflow module, we don't provide a form builder for the workflow. The forms are left for the registered modules to define their own forms. Here we set a link to the page that will handle the workflow form. When workflow instances are created, the Workflow module will call this page and send to it the current step and the variables' values.

The Available fields set the availability period of the workflow definition. In some cases, the workflow will work only in a specific period; in this case, the user will be able to set the dates for the availability period.

Steps

The second tab is Steps (Figure 11-5), which lists the steps in the workflow and enables the user to manage them by searching, viewing, adding, modifying, or deleting steps.

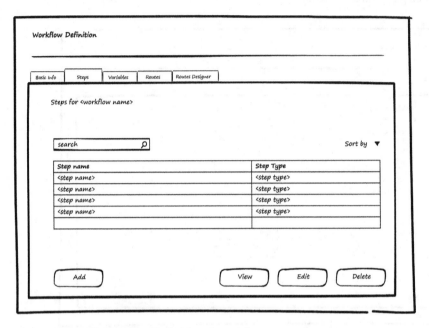

Figure 11-5. Edit Workflow Definition: Steps tab

From the Steps page, the user can select an existing step and view, edit, or delete it, or add a new step. Figure 11-6 shows the Step Editor page, which contains two tabs: Basic Info and Associated Tasks. The Basic Info tab contains the step and description. Two important features can set by the user:

- *Allow Returning to Previous Step*: If this feature is selected, the user who performs the task associated with this step in a workflow instance can return the workflow instance to the previous step.

- *Allow Returning to Initiator*: If this feature is selected, the user who performs the task associated with this step in a workflow instance will be able to return the workflow instance to the initiator. There are two possibilities after the initiator performs the task returned to them: the system can make the workflow go in the normal flow from the initiation step, or it can make the workflow go directly to the step from which the workflow instance was returned.

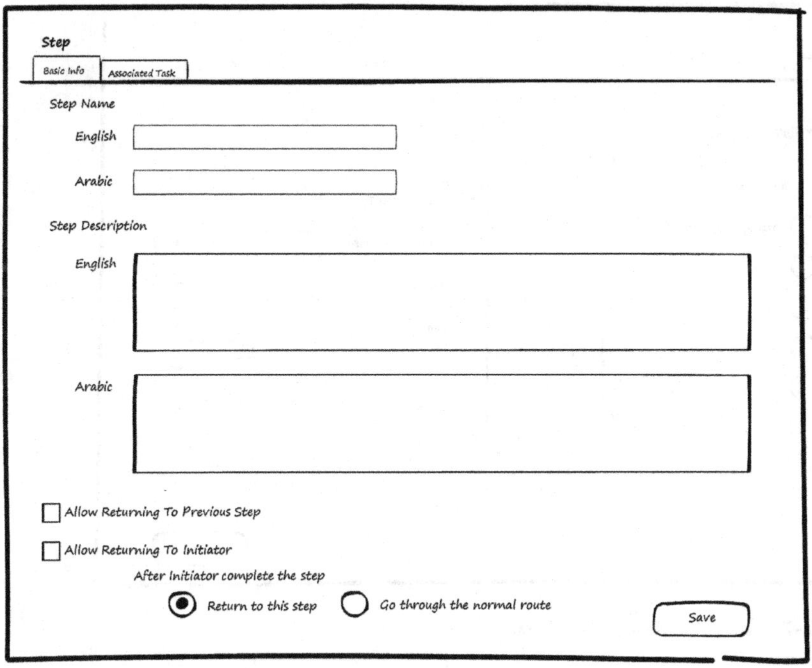

Step

| Basic Info | Associated Task |

Step Name

English [   ]

Arabic [   ]

Step Description

English [   ]

Arabic [   ]

☐ Allow Returning To Previous Step

☐ Allow Returning To Initiator

After Initiator complete the step

⦿ Return to this step ◯ Go through the normal route

(Save)

Figure 11-6. *Edit Step: Basic Info*

The second tab, Associated Task, shown in Figure 11-7, is used to define the task that will be assigned for this step. The task will have a type, which comes from the registered task types. The task types that are mostly used with workflow are Review, Decision, Inspection, Payment, and Custom.

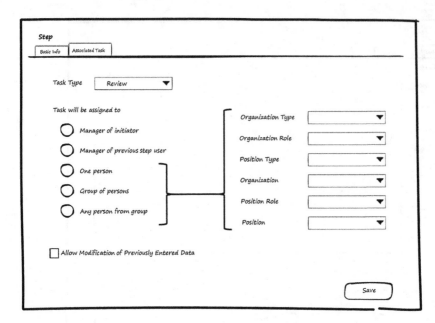

Figure 11-7. *Edit Step: Associated Task*

Here, the user can set parameters that will determine to whom the system will assign the task. It can be assigned to the manager of the initiator or the manager of the user who performs the previous step. Or it can be assigned to a person or group of persons, or to a person from a group. For those options, the user must set some values to allow the system to be able to find the person or the group that the task will be assigned. These values to be set can be any of the following: Organization Type, Organization Role, Position Type, Organization, Position Role, or Position.

For example, assume the user selects the task to be assigned to a group and then selects an Organization. The system will assign the task to all employees working in this Organization. The user can reduce the set by also setting the value for the Position Type. In this case, the system will assign the task to all employees with the selected Position Type who work in the selected Organization.

Variables

The third tab, Variables, shown in Figure 11-8, is used to list the variables defined for the workflow and enables the user to manage them by searching, viewing, adding, modifying, or deleting variables.

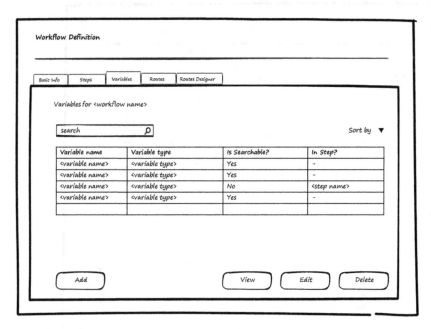

Figure 11-8. *Edit Workflow Definition: Variables*

Figure 11-9 shows the Variable Editor page where the user can set the name and type of the variable. A variable can be searchable and in this case will have a display name (if we have a page to search for workflow instances based on variable values, the searchable variables will appear in it).

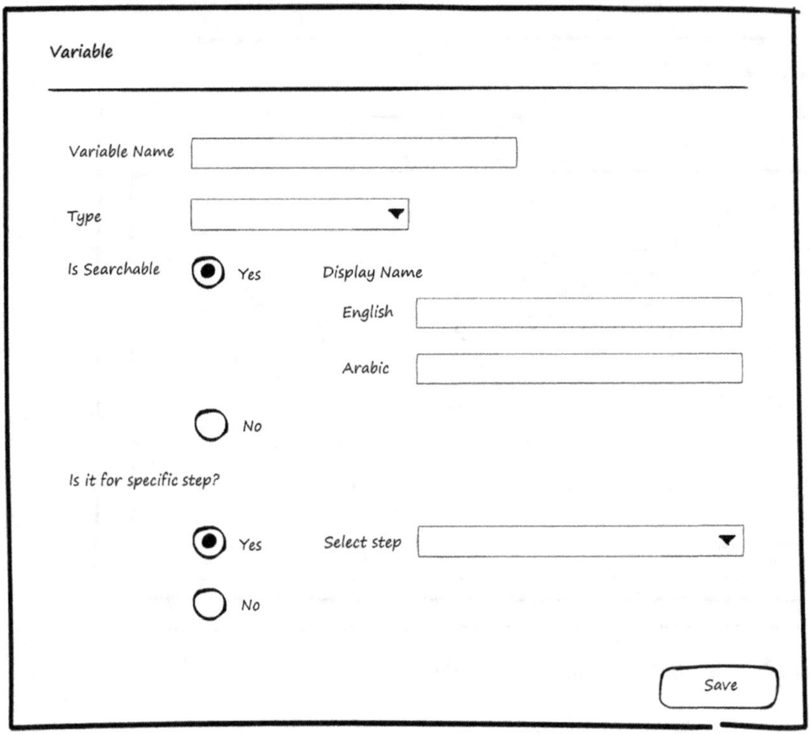

Figure 11-9. Edit Variable

A variable may be used only with a specific step, so there is an option for the user to associate the variable with a specific step.

Routes

The Fourth tab shown back in Figure 11-10 is Routes, which lists the routes defined for the workflow and enables the user to manage them by searching, viewing, adding, modifying, or deleting routes.

144

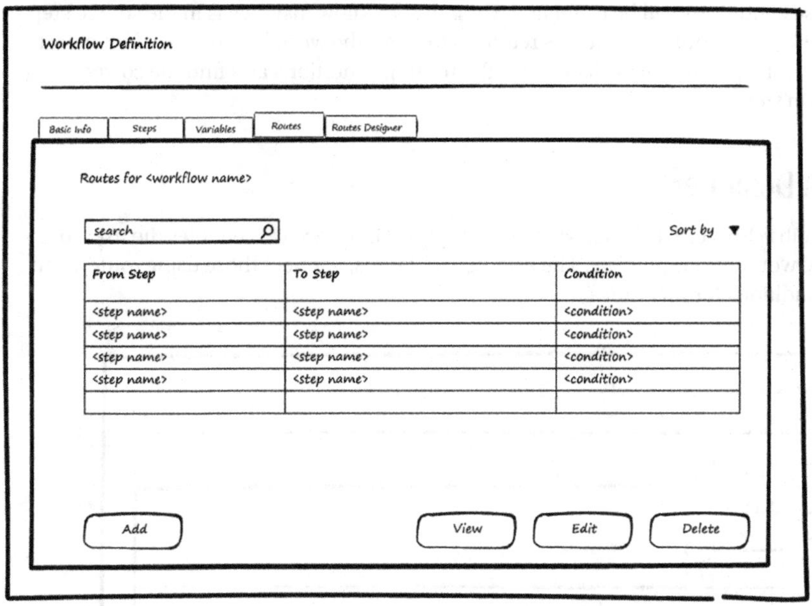

Figure 11-10. *Edit workflow definition: Routes*

The Route Editor page is shown in Figure 11-11. In this page, the user can set the source and destination step for the route. In addition, the user can define the conditions for this route based on the workflow's variables values. The comparison can be any of the following: equal to, not equal to, greater than, greater than or equal, less than, less than or equal, between, in, not in.

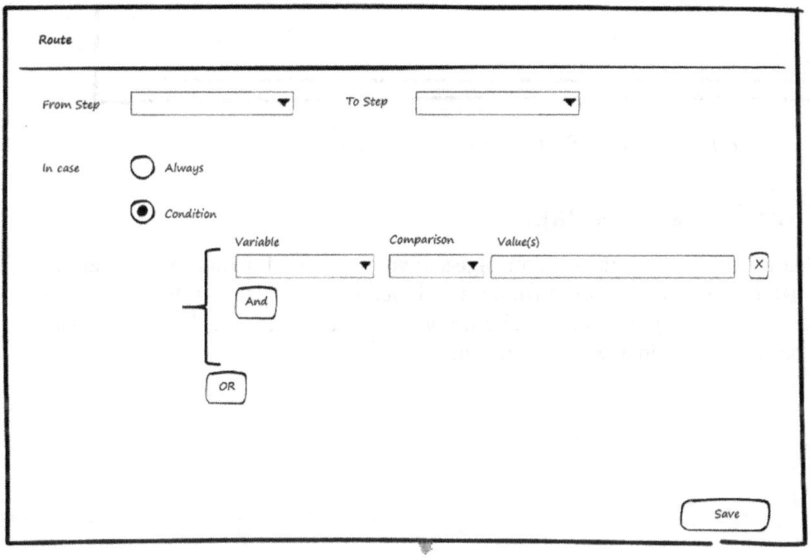

Figure 11-11. *Edit Route*

These conditions will be evaluated when the workflow instance is in the source step and its tasks are completed, and it is required to move the workflow instance to the next step. The Workflow module will evaluate the routing conditions and find the correct destination step.

Routes Designer

The fifth tab is Routes Designer, which is a graphical interface that enables the user to create the workflow graphically. The user can add steps, connect those using routes, and define conditions for the routes.

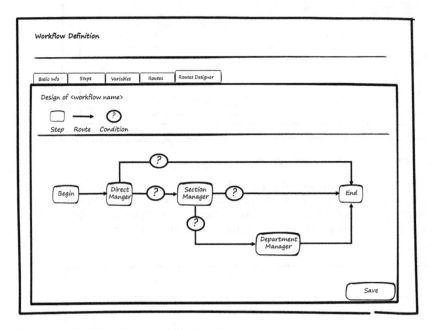

Figure 11-12. *Edit Workflow Definition: Routes Designer*

Workflow Instances Page

The Workflow Instances administration page shown in Figure 11-13 allows the user to view the instances of the workflow instances and their status. It also lets the user view the path and the workflow instance data. Another important feature is that the user can reassign the active tasks in a workflow instance.

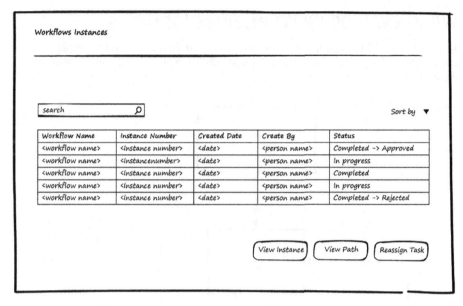

Figure 11-13. *Manage Workflows Instances*

When user chooses to reassign a task, the system displays the Reassign Tasks Page shown in Figure 11-14. This page lists all the active tasks in the workflow instance and to whom these tasks are assigned. The user can then reassign the tasks to other persons and write comments for them.

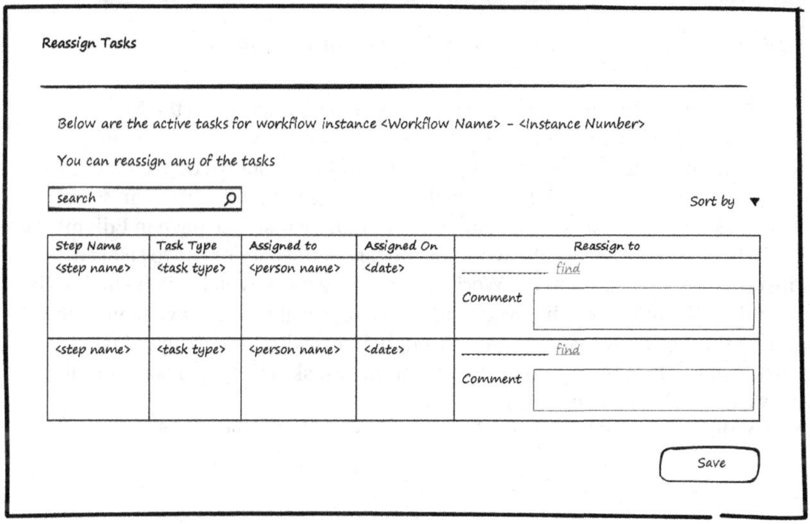

Figure 11-14. *Reassign Tasks*

Workflow Module Wireframes for Users

In this section of the chapter, you will see high-level wireframe screens for the pages used by normal users to create and track workflows instances. The UI flow is shown in Figure 11-15.

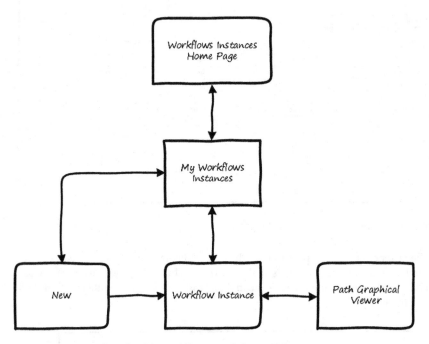

Figure 11-15. *UI flow for the Workflows module: Workflows Instances*

From the Workflows Instances home page, the user can navigate to the My Workflows Instances page, which lets them create a new workflow instance or get information about the status of the currently active workflow instance they created. To create a new instance, the system will display the New page where the user can select the workflow, and then the system will display the Workflow Instance page in Edit mode. To view and get information about the workflow instance, the user needs to select a workflow instance and navigates to the Workflow Instance page, which will be in the View mode. From this page, the user can navigate to Path Graphical Viewer page to view the actual path that the workflow instance goes through. Users who have assigned tasks in the workflow instance will be able to find and perform these tasks from the Tasks module (in the same way as explained in Chapter 10).

The rest of this section will go through wireframes for the pages described.

My Workflows Instances Page

Figure 11-16 shows the My Workflows Instances page, which enables any user to manage their workflows instances. Users can search their workflows instances, view a workflow instance to track its status, view the path that the workflow instance goes through, and create new workflows instances. There is a link to the My Tasks page that leads the user to the Tasks page where they can perform any task assigned to them in any workflow instance.

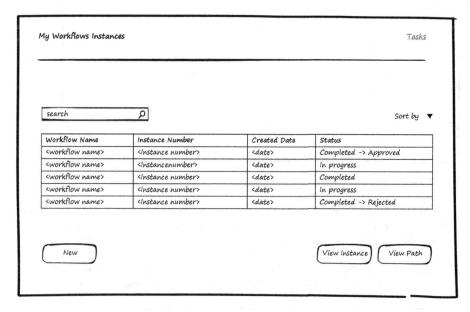

Figure 11-16. *Manage My Workflows Instances*

New Workflow Instance Page

When the user clicks the New button in the My Workflows Instances page, the system displays the New Workflow Instance Page shown in Figure 11-17. This page displays the existing workflows of which the user has permission to create instances. The workflows are grouped based on their categories.

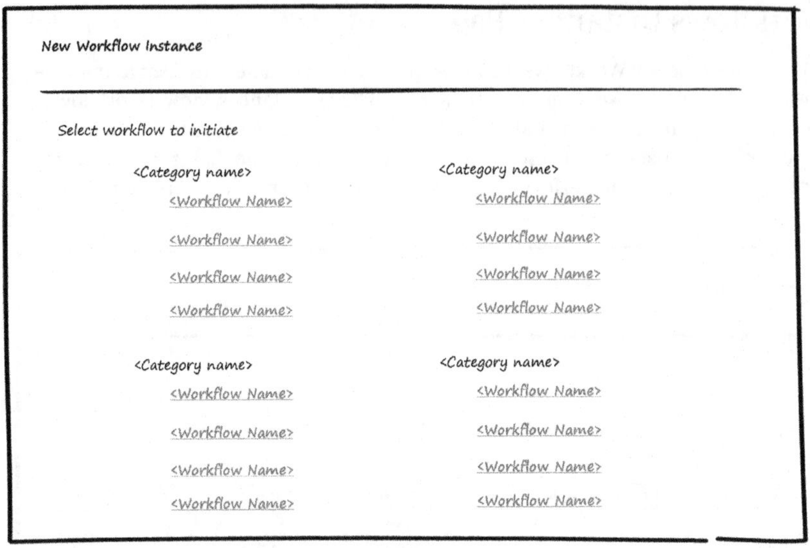

New Workflow Instance

Select workflow to initiate

<Category name>   <Category name>
    <Workflow Name>   <Workflow Name>

    <Workflow Name>   <Workflow Name>

    <Workflow Name>   <Workflow Name>

    <Workflow Name>   <Workflow Name>

<Category name>   <Category name>
    <Workflow Name>   <Workflow Name>

    <Workflow Name>   <Workflow Name>

    <Workflow Name>   <Workflow Name>

    <Workflow Name>   <Workflow Name>

Figure 11-17. *Choose New Workflow Instance*

After selecting the workflow, the Workflow module will call the page that was defined in the workflow definition to be displayed inside the new Workflow Instance page, as shown in Figure 11-18. The page will receive parameters with the current step (which is the begin step). The module that registered this workflow will then display the workflow form and validate it after being called by the Workflow module when the user clicks Send. The Workflows module will then handle the routing for the workflow instance.

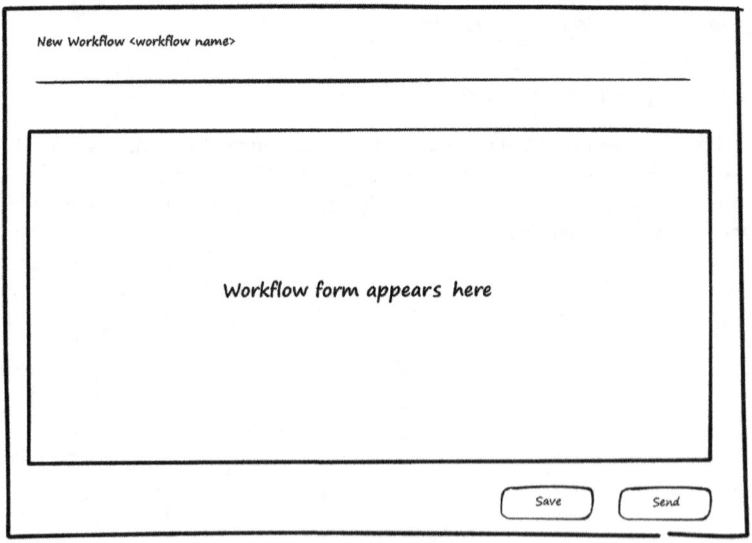

New Workflow <workflow name>

Workflow form appears here

Save   Send

Figure 11-18. *Fill form of the new workflow instance*

Path Graphical Viewer Page

From the My Workflow Instances page, the user can choose to view the path. The system will display the Path Viewer page shown in Figure 11-19. The workflow steps are listed in the left. The system shows the flow of tasks around these steps on the right. A task can be reassigned, or the user can choose return the task to the previous step. In this case, a new task is created for the previous step again. The user can track the workflow instance from the Path Viewer page.

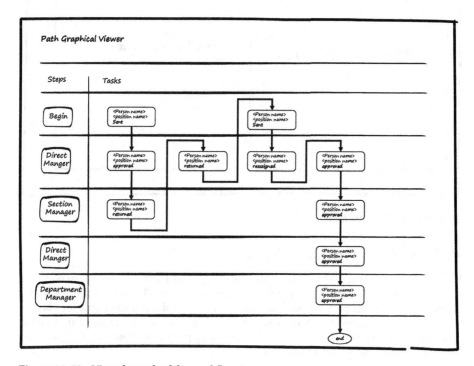

Figure 11-19. *View the path of the workflow instance*

Workflow Instance Viewer Page

The page in Figure 11-20 is used to view the workflow instance. It will display the data in the workflow instance form and the list of tasks assigned to users to perform. For each task, comments, decisions, or actions done by the user will be shown.

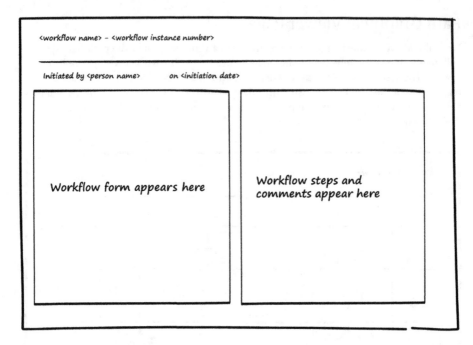

Figure 11-20. *View workflow instance*

Performing a Workflow Task

When the Workflow module routes a workflow and assigns a task to a user based on the step definition, the task will appear in the user's My Tasks page. To perform the task, the system will display the page based on its type. Figure 11-21 shows a wireframe for a task of type Decision. It enables the user to view the workflow instance (data and actions done on it). At the bottom of the page is the task-performing panel. For a Decision task, the user will be able to approve or reject and enter comments.

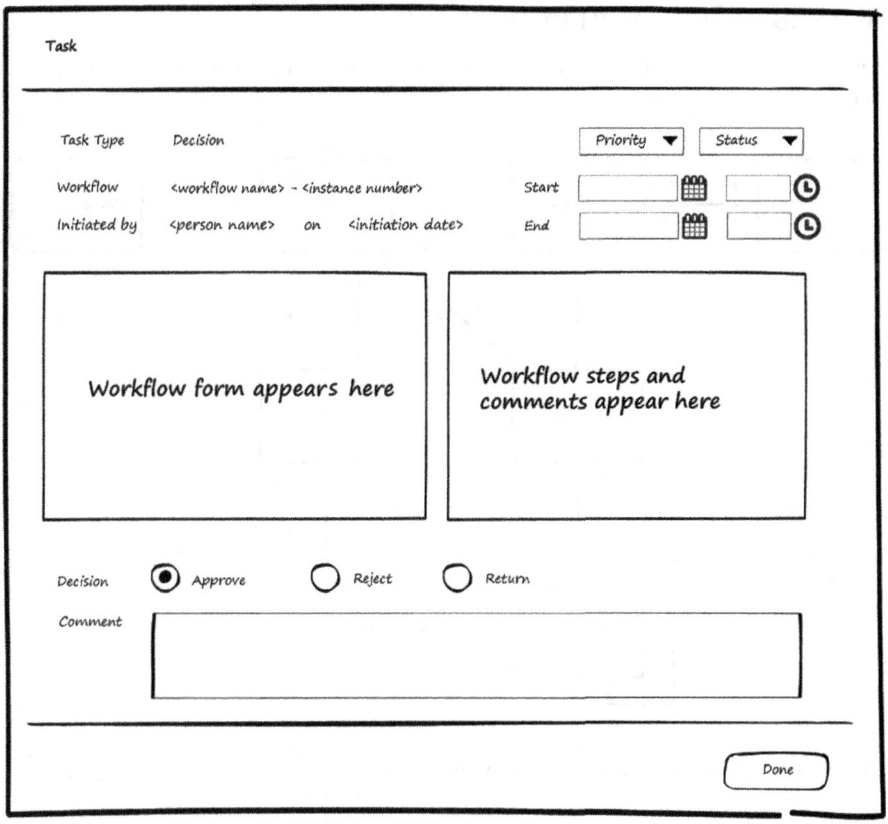

Figure 11-21. *Perform workflow task*

Workflow Module Entities

Now that you've seen use-cases and wireframes for the Workflow module, let's look at the entities used by the Workflow module to store the information needed to manage workflows. This section is divided into two sub-sections—the first is for entities used to define workflow, and the second is for entities used for workflow instances.

Workflow Definition Entities

Figure 11-22 shows the entities used for workflow definition and the relations between them.

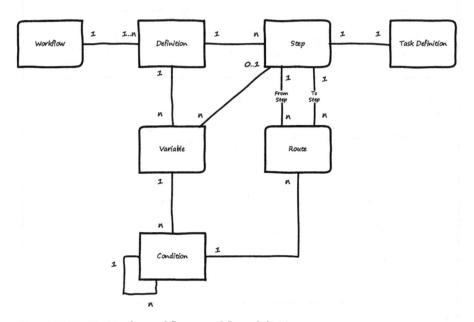

Figure 11-22. *Entities for workflows: workflows definition*

Here is a description for each entity:

- *Workflow*: Stores the main information about the workflow.

- *Definition*: Stores and tracks workflow definition versions.

- *Variable*: Stores the definition of the variables used with the workflow version.

- *Step*: Stores the workflow's steps.

- *Route*: Stores the routes among the steps.

- *Condition*: Stores the conditions that need to be true for the routes.

- *Task Definition*: Stores the definition of the tasks that will be associated with the steps.

The relations between these entities can be summarized as follows:

- Workflow can have multiple definitions (each definition represent a version of the workflow).

- Workflow definition can have multiple Variables.

- Workflow Definition has multiple Steps.

- Each Step can have Variables associated with it.

- Each Step has a Task Definition.

- Two Steps are connected together using Route.

- Route can have one condition.

- Condition can be used with many Routes.

- Condition can consist of many sub-conditions.

Workflow Instances Entities

Figure 11-23 shows the entities used for workflow instances and the relations between them.

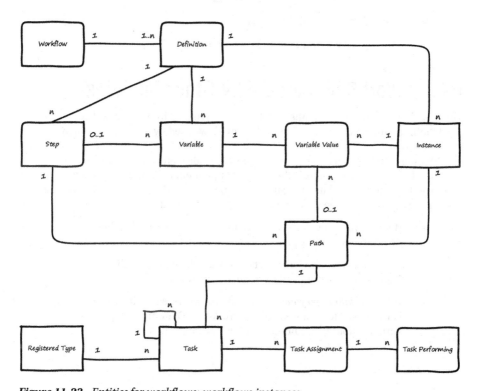

Figure 11-23. *Entities for workflows: workflows instances*

Here is a description for each entity:

- *Instance*: Stores created instances of workflows definitions.

- *Variable Value*: Stores values of variables used with workflow instances.

- *Path*: Stores information about steps sequence that the workflow were routed through.

- *Task*: Stores tasks created for the workflow instances.

- *Task Assignment*: Stores information about whom the tasks are assigned for.

The relations between these entities can be summarized as follows:

- Multiple Instances can be created from one workflow definition.

- Instance will have multiple Variable Values.

- Variable in the workflow definition will have values associated with the workflow Instances.

- Variable Value can be associated with a workflow Path.

- One Step can appear many times in the Path.

- One Path can have multiple Tasks.

- Task can have multiple Task Assignments.

Use of Workflow Module by Other Modules

The Workflow module accepts other modules to be plugged into it, to enable managing the definitions and creating instances of the workflows used by the module which registered to.

Modules can be plugged into the Workflow module using the register workflow use-case. In order to be registered, they should implement the register workflow interface. The interface will need the module to be registered to be able to answer the following questions, and the answer will be used to fill the entities as described:

- *Who are you?* The answer to this question will be saved in the Registered Module entity.

- *What task types do you use?* The answer will be saved in the Registered Types entity described in Chapter 10.

- *What workflows do you use?* The answer will be saved in the entities used to define workflow (Workflow, Definition, Step, Variable, Route, Condition, and Task Definition).

After a module is plugged into the Workflow module, the module that requested the registration can use the register workflow definition use-case to register new workflow, the update workflow definition use-case to add a new version to a defined workflow, and the get workflow instance status use-case to inquire about workflow instance status.

Summary

This chapter discussed the Workflow module, including what workflows are, their task types, and workflows instances. I discussed use-cases for the Workflow module and showed wireframes for the screens. You saw the entities and their relations, and I talked about how other modules could use the Workflow module.

CHAPTER 12

■ ■ ■

Notifications Module

Persons who use a software system need to be notified about occasional actions they should perform in the system—for example, renewing a subscription when it expires. They may need also to be notified about results of actions they performed, or about updates in a part in the system they're interested in. This means every software system should be flexible in allowing users to choose what they want to be notified about and which notification methods they prefer. The Notifications module's main functionality is to manage subscription to notification topics and notify interested persons.

After finishing this chapter, you will be able to answer the following questions:

- What is notification?

- Why is notification required?

- How should you store notifications?

- What does the UI for the Notifications module look like?

Notification is about sending messages to users to inform them about something. This message can be sent by various methods:

- E-mail

- SMS

- Phone call

- Message in web browser

- Social media

There are two types of notifications:

- *Out notifications*: This is when the system sends notifications to persons or to other systems.

- *In notifications*: This is when persons or other systems send notifications to our system.

This chapter focuses on out notifications to persons. Note that notification messages may be sent directly to a person—or they can be sent to an organization where there is a person who will be responsible for it. In that case, we need to have use-cases and

© Mohamed Farouk 2017
M. Farouk, *Infrastructure Software Modules for Enterprises*,
DOI 10.1007/978-1-4842-3021-3_12

wireframes for the organization notification, which is similar to the direct-to-person notification discussed in this chapter.

Importance of Notifications

Users (persons) need to be notified about changes happening in the system. These changes may affect the persons using the system or associated with it. Notifications may be grouped under topics, which means there will be topics in the system, and business or system modules use these topics. Every module will be sending notifications to persons about changes in the topics that the module is responsible for.

Notifications help persons know what is going on in the system for the topics they are affected by and keep them up to date about the tasks, requests, or results affecting them. The Notifications module help the users manage notifications by choosing their preferred notification method for different topics. It also helps other modules register their topics and send notifications for the related persons.

Notification Module Use-Cases

The Notifications module is responsible for managing and sending notifications. Figure 12-1 shows use-cases for the Notifications module. Actors for these use-cases are the user who has permission to manage a topic's definition, any person who is related to the topic of the notification, any user who uses the system, and the system module, which can be a business module or infrastructure module that needs to register its topics or send notifications to persons.

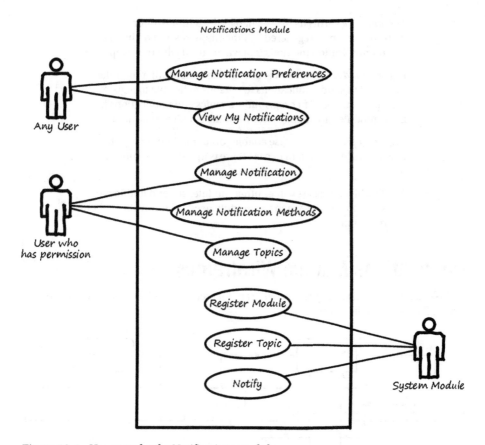

Figure 12-1. *Use-cases for the Notifications module*

Here is a description for each use-case:

- *Manage notification preferences*: This use-case enables the user to set the preferred notification methods for the topics allowed for them in the system.

- *View my notifications*: This use-case enables the user to see what notifications have been sent to them and what the notification method was.

- *Manage notifications*: This use-case enables the administrator to see notifications sent by the system and determine whether there was any failure in delivering the notification messages.

- *Manage notification methods*: This use-case enables the administrator to define the notifications methods in the system and the plugins that will handle these methods.

- *Manage topics*: This use-case enables the administrator to manage the topics registered by other modules and define the default notification methods that will be used with these topics.

- *Register module*: This use-case is used to enable other modules that need to send notifications to persons to be able to register their information. After registration, topics and notifications by those modules are manageable from the Notifications module.

- *Register topic*: This use-case enables other modules to register new topics in the system in case there is update to the module topics.

- *Notify*: This use-case enables other modules to send notification messages to persons when the module needs to notify them about a certain topic.

Notifications Module Wireframes

In this section, you will see high-level wireframe screens for the Notifications module. The UI flow is shown in Figure 12-2.

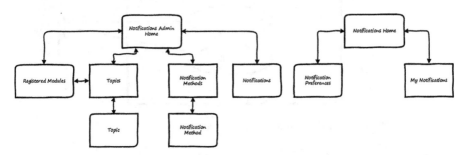

Figure 12-2. *UI flow for the Notifications module*

The Notifications module is divided into two parts, one for the administrator and the other for the normal users. In Figure 12-2, the administrator UI flow is shown in the left side of the diagram, and the normal user UI flow is shown on the right.

- *Administrator UI flow*: From the home page of the notifications admin, the user can navigate to the Registered Modules page to see what modules have been registered. From the Registered Module page or the home page, the user can navigate to the Topics page to manage the topics used by each registered module. The user can search, view, modify, or add topics. From the Topics page the user can navigate to the Topic page, which lets the user view, add, or edit a topic. It's also possible from the home page to navigate to the Notifications Methods page to manage the notification methods. Adding, editing, or viewing notification methods can be done by navigating to the Notification Method page. If the admin wants to see the notifications that have been sent or will be sent by the system, they can navigate from the home page to the Notifications page.

- *Normal user UI flow*: From the home page for the normal user, the user can navigate to the Notification Preferences page to define their preferences for notification about the registered topics in the system. In addition, the user can navigate to the My Notifications page to see information about all notifications sent to them from the system.

In the rest of this section, you will see what these pages look like.

Notification Methods Page

The Notification Methods page displays the method and the *executer*. Every notification method has an executer to do the notification. For example, if the notification method is e-mail, the executer will be the class in the system that contains the code responsible for sending e-mail messages. The user can add, edit, or delete a notification method. Figure 12-3 shows the Notification Methods page.

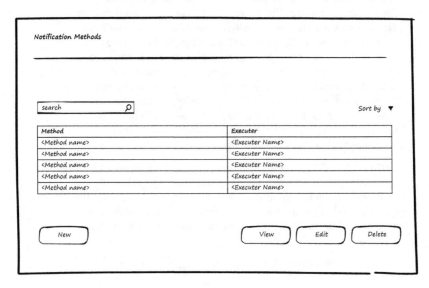

Figure 12-3. *Manage Notification Methods*

Notification Method Page

In Figure 12-4, you see a wireframe for the Notification Method page in edit mode, which can be used to edit or add a notification method. As mentioned, a notification method has a name and an executer, and the executer should be a file that contains a class to handle the notifications done by this method.

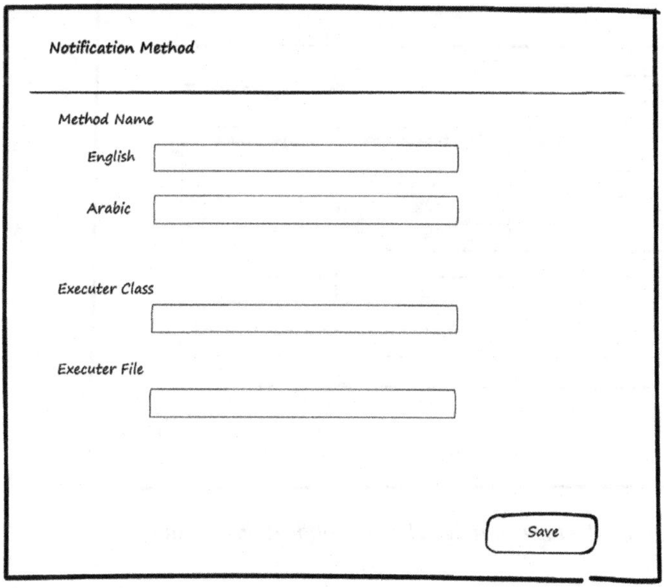

Figure 12-4. *Edit Notification Method*

The Notification Method page depends on the Localization module to support entering the notification method name in the supported languages.

Registered Modules Page

When other modules are registered (plugged) into the Notifications module, they will appear in the Registered Module page. From this page, the user can manage the topics used by those modules. Figure 12-5 shows a wireframe for listing the registered modules.

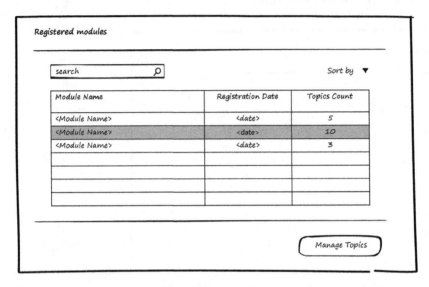

Figure 12-5. *Registered modules to be managed by the Notifications module*

Topics Page

The Topics page displays the topics used in a certain module. A topic has a registration date and may be a sub-topic or have a parent topic. The user can add, edit, or delete topics. Figure 12-6 shows the Topics page.

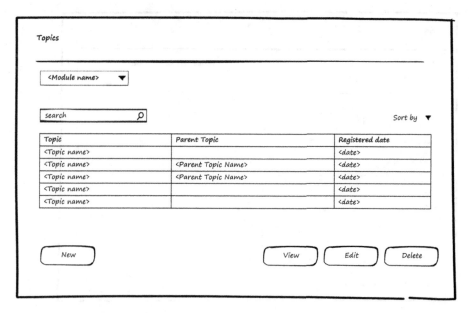

Figure 12-6. *Manage Topics*

Topic Page

Figure 12-7 shows a wireframe for the Topic page in edit mode, which can be used for editing or adding a topic. A topic has a name, code, description, and default notification methods (from the Notification Preferences page, the user can override these defaults).

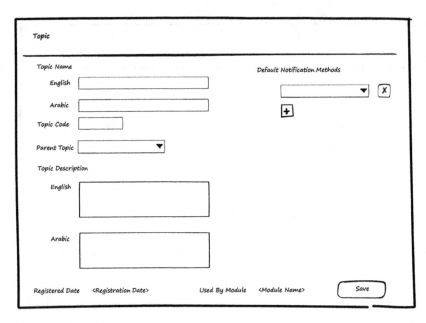

Figure 12-7. *Edit Topic*

The Topic page depends on the Localization module to support entering the topic name and description in the supported languages.

Notifications Page

The Notifications page displays all notifications sent or to be sent by the system. It allows the administrator to monitor the status of notification messages, whether they have been sent or are still in the queue.

Figure 12-8 shows a wireframe for the Notifications page.

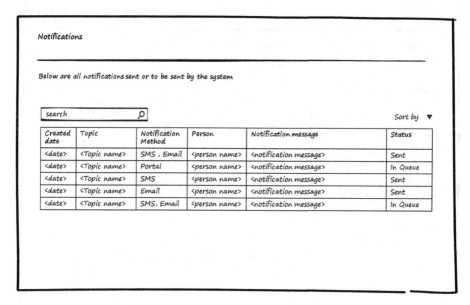

Figure 12-8. *List Notifications*

Notification Preferences Page

In Figure 12-9, you can see a wireframe for the Notification Preferences page. This page allows choosing a topic and then defining the preferences for receiving notification messages about this topic. The user can choose not to receive any messages or can specify the notification methods to be used to be notified about the topic. In both cases, the notification messages sent to the user can be viewed from the My Notifications page.

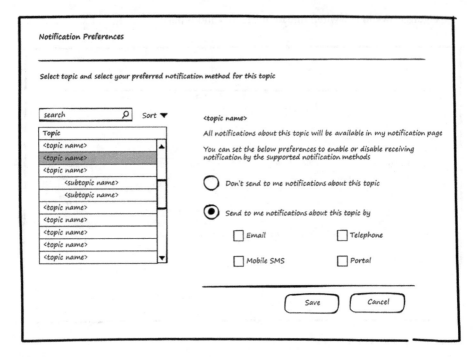

Figure 12-9. *Manage Notification Preferences*

My Notifications Page

The My Notifications page displays to the user all notifications sent to them. Figure 12-10 shows a wireframe for the My Notifications page.

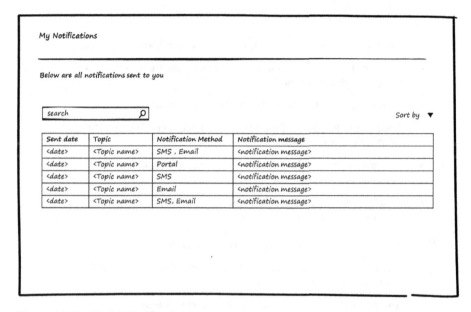

My Notifications

Below are all notifications sent to you

| search | | | | | Sort by ▼ |

Sent date	Topic	Notification Method	Notification message
<date>	<Topic name>	SMS , Email	<notification message>
<date>	<Topic name>	Portal	<notification message>
<date>	<Topic name>	SMS	<notification message>
<date>	<Topic name>	Email	<notification message>
<date>	<Topic name>	SMS, Email	<notification message>

Figure 12-10. *List My Notifications*

Notifications Module Entities

You've now seen use-cases and wireframes for the Notifications module. It's time to talk about the entities used by the Notifications module to store the information needed to manage notifications. Figure 12-11 shows the entities and the relations between them.

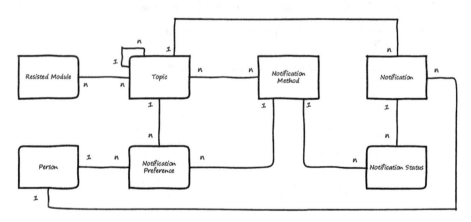

Figure 12-11. *Entities for the Notifications module*

Here is a description for each entity:

- *Notification Method*: Stores the data for the Notification method.

- *Registered Module*: Stores data for modules that are registered to use the Notifications module.

- *Topic*: Stores the topics used by the registered modules.

- *Notification Preference*: Stores the preferences of each person for notifications about topics.

- *Notification*: Stores the notification messages to be sent to persons.

- *Notification Status*: Stores the status of the notification messages (such as *in queue*, *sent*, or *failed*).

The relations between these entities can be summarized as follows:

- The Registered module can notify about multiple Topics, and Topics can belong to multiple modules.

- Topic can have sub-topics under them, and sub-topic can be under only one Topic.

- Notification Method can be used as the default notification method with multiple Topics.

- One Topic can have multiple default Notification Methods.

- Topic can have many notification messages sent for it.

- Every notification message can have multiple statuses (one for each notification method used to deliver the message)

- Persons can define multiple Notification Preferences based on the Topics.

- Persons can receive many notification messages.

Use of the Notification Module by Other Modules

The Notification module accepts other modules to be plugged into it to enable managing notifications sent under the topics used by the module that is to be registered.

Modules can be plugged into the Notifications module using the register module use-case. In order to be registered, they should implement the register module interface. The interface will need the module to be registered to be able to answer the following questions, and the answer will be used to fill the entities as described:

- *Who are you?* The answer to this question will be saved in Registered Module entity.

- *What topics do you have?* The answer will be saved in the Topic entity.

- *What are the default notification methods for each topic?* The answer will be saved in the Topic entity.

After a module is plugged into the Notifications module, the module that requests the registration can use the notify use-case to send notification messages to persons.

Summary

This chapter discussed the Notifications module, including what notifications are and why they are required. I discussed use-cases for the Notifications module and showed wireframes for the screens. You were introduced to the entities and their relations, and you saw how other modules could use the Notifications module.

CHAPTER 13

■ ■ ■

Follow-Up Module

Persons using a software system may need to be reminded to do something about a record saved in the system. Based on this reminder, they will perform actions that may be inside the system or outside it. An example of an action to be performed outside the system would be making a call to inquire about an item that will be delivered from an external organization. This means the software system should be flexible in allowing users to select any record and ask the system to remind them about it within a certain time. The Follow-Up module's main functionality is to manage these follow-ups by allowing users to create reminder requests on data records and receive notifications for these data records.

After finishing this chapter, you will be able to answer the following questions:

- What is follow-up?

- How should you store follow-up data?

- What does the UI for the Follow-Up module look like?

System users are often interested in some data in the system and need to be reminded about this data after a period of time. The user can choose to repeat the reminder or stop receiving reminders. That's what follow-up is about—sending a reminder to a user at a specific time defined by the user.

© Mohamed Farouk 2017
M. Farouk, *Infrastructure Software Modules for Enterprises*,
DOI 10.1007/978-1-4842-3021-3_13

Follow-Up Module Use-Cases

Figure 13-1 shows use-cases for the Follow-Up module. Actors for these use-cases are any users authorized in the system.

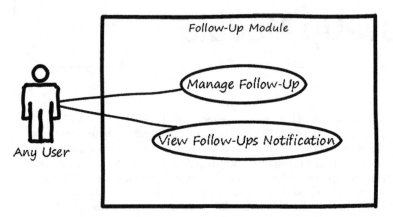

Figure 13-1. *Use-cases for the Follow-Up module*

Here is a description for each use-case:

- *Manage follow-up*: This use-case is used to enable the user to create or update a follow-up item.

- *View follow-Ups notification*: This use-case is used to enable the user to view the follow-up notifications sent to them by the system.

Follow-Up Module Wireframes

In this section of the chapter, you will see high-level wireframe screens for the Follow-Up module. The UI flow is shown in Figure 13-2.

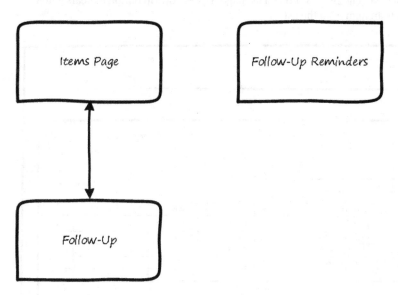

Figure 13-2. *UI flow for the Follow-Up module*

The Follow-Up page can be reached from any page in the system that displays a list of items. When a user selects an item, they can make a follow-up on this item. The Follow-Up reminders page can be reached from anyplace in the system and will be shown automatically at the reminder time. Alternatively, a user can access the page from the top of any page in the system.

Follow-Up Page

The Follow-Up page can be opened from any page that displays an item of any type. When run, the Follow-Up module should display the Follow Up button on the list page and the detail page. Figure 13-3 shows a list page. The Follow Up button appears when the user selects an item from the list.

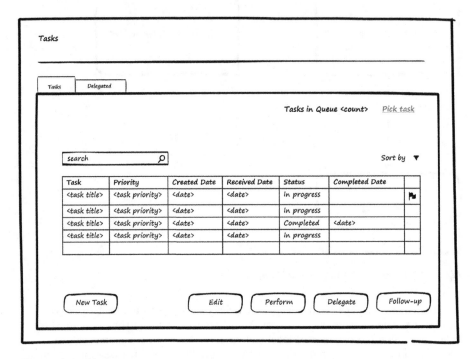

Figure 13-3. *List page*

When the Follow Up button is clicked, the Follow-Up Editor page is displayed. Figure 13-4 shows a wireframe for this page. The user can enter text as a flag and select the time for a reminder. When the follow-up is saved, a flag appears near the item in the list as shown in Figure 13-3 (the flag in the last column). The follow-up can be removed by clicking the Clear Flag button in the Follow-Up Editor page.

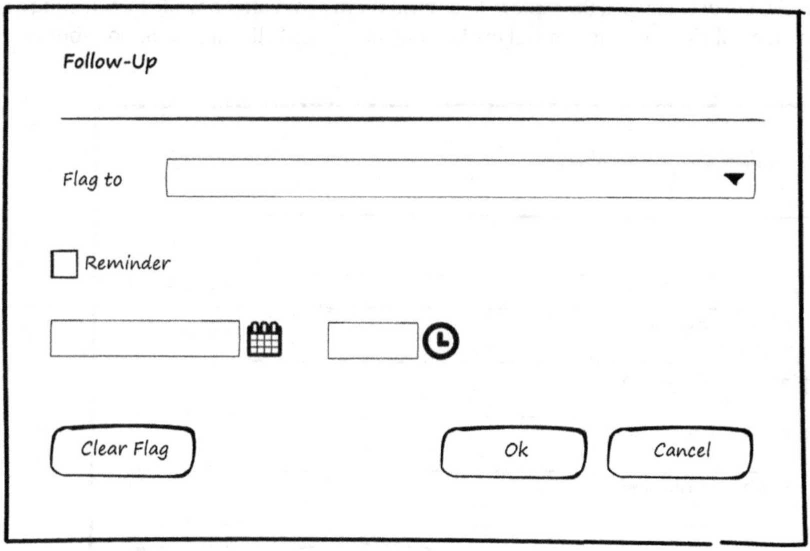

Figure 13-4. Edit Follow-Up

Follow-Up Reminders Page

The system will display a reminder page for the follow-ups when their reminder time comes. Figure 13-5 shows a wireframe for the Reminders page. This page shows the items that have follow-ups with the flag text (<Flag to text>) below each item, and Overdue is based on the reminder time. The user can select an item and dismiss the reminder for it. Alternatively, the user can ask the system to remind them again after a while by selecting a value from the "Click Snooze to remind me in" drop-down and clicking the Snooze button.

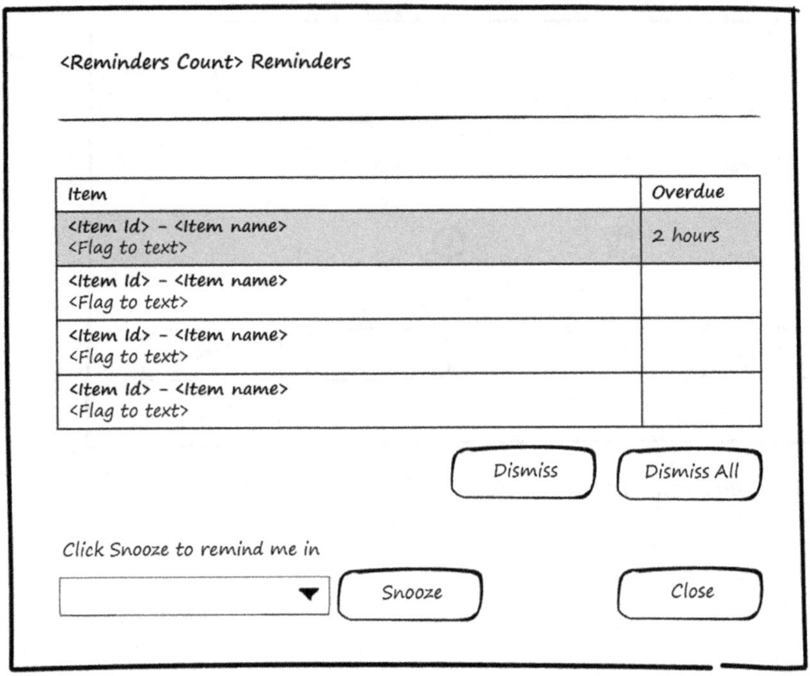

<Reminders Count> Reminders

Item	Overdue
<Item Id> – <Item name> <Flag to text>	2 hours
<Item Id> – <Item name> <Flag to text>	
<Item Id> – <Item name> <Flag to text>	
<Item Id> – <Item name> <Flag to text>	

Dismiss   Dismiss All

Click Snooze to remind me in

▼   Snooze   Close

Figure 13-5. Edit follow-up reminders

Follow-Up Module Entities

You've seen use-cases and wireframes for the Follow-Up module. Now it's time to see the entities used by the Follow-Up module to store the information needed to manage follow-ups. Figure 13-6 shows the entities and the relations between them.

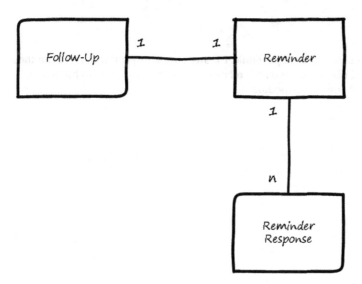

Figure 13-6. *Entities for the Follow-Up module*

Here is a description for each entity:

- *Follow-Up*: Stores the follow-up data (item and flag text).

- *Reminder*: Stores the reminder time for the follow-up.

- *Reminder Response*: Stores the data for the user response to the reminder.

The relations between these entities can be summarized as follows:

- An item can have only one Follow-Up.

- Follow-Up must have one Reminder.

- Reminder can have many Reminder Responses.

Use of the Follow-Up Module by Other Modules

Other modules don't need to register to use the Follow-Up module. The Follow-Up module will inject itself in the UI layer and will append the required features to enable follow-up.

Summary

This chapter discussed the Follow-Up module. I showed use-cases and wireframes for the screens and discussed the entities and their relations. In last section, you saw how other modules could use the Follow-Up module.

CHAPTER 14

■ ■ ■

Payments Module

Most organizations, especially for-profit companies, provide paid services for persons who deal with them. Every person needs to pay invoices that the organization issued for them. This means the software system should be flexible in defining methods to collect payments and allowing persons to pay their invoices. The Payments module's main functionality is to enable software systems to manage payments for invoices.

After finishing this chapter, you will be able to answer the following questions:

- What to pay for?

- What are payment methods?

- How should you store payment data?

- What does the UI for the Payments module look like?

Most organizations provide services, and these services usually require fees to be paid by consumers. The Payments module is responsible for handling the payment for the services, and business modules in the system are responsible for these services. The business modules generate invoices to consumers, and then the Payments module handles how these invoices will be paid by the consumer.

Different payment methods can be used—for example, online payment gateway, swipe device payment, bank transfer, check, cash, and more. The Payments module is responsible for allowing users to pay with different methods based on their permissions. For example, the customer can pay invoices online through a payment gateway—or they can go to the premises of the organization and pay money to an authorized employee who has permission to collect the payment by other methods. The employee could collect the money in cash and mark the invoice as paid in cash, or could receive a check from the customer, mark the invoice as paid by check, and enter the check information in the system. All these actions will be done through the Payments module.

Invoices can be paid fully or partially, and the Payments module will manage this information. Other modules that generate the invoices can inquire about the invoice's payment status.

© Mohamed Farouk 2017

M. Farouk, *Infrastructure Software Modules for Enterprises*,
DOI 10.1007/978-1-4842-3021-3_14

Payments Module Use-Cases

Figure 14-1 shows use-cases for the Payments module. Actors for these use-cases include any user of the system who has invoices to pay for, employees who use the system to collect money for invoices created for any person (or user), an administrator who defines the payment methods, and the system modules that generate invoices to be paid by the consumer.

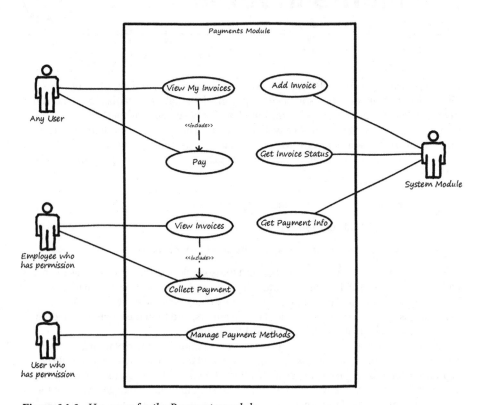

Figure 14-1. *Use-cases for the Payments module*

Here is a description for each use-case:

- *Manage payment methods*: This use-case enables the admin user to add, delete, and modify payment methods that will be used to pay the invoices.

- *View my invoices*: This use-case enables the user to search and view the invoices created for them. They can also pay any unpaid invoice.

- *Pay*: This use-case enables the user to pay an invoice. It's a use-case included in the view my invoices use-case.

- *View invoices*: This use-case enables the user who has permission to search and view all invoices created for any person or user. They can also collect payment for any unpaid invoice.

- *Collect payment*: This use-case enables the user who has permission to collect payment for any invoice. It's a use-case included in the view invoices use-case. The user will have more payment options than the options in the pay use-case.

- *Add invoice*: This use-case enables other modules to add invoices to be managed for payment by the Payments module.

- *Get invoice status*: This use-case enables other modules to make inquiries for their added invoices to check the payment status (not paid, partially paid, and paid).

- *Get payment info*: This use-case enables other modules to get information about the invoice payment (what the payment method was, date of payment, and more).

Payments Module Wireframes

This section shows high-level wireframe screens for the Payments module. The UI flow is shown in Figure 14-2.

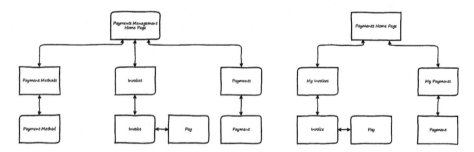

Figure 14-2. *UI flow for the Payments module*

The Payments module consists of two parts. The first part is *payments management*, used by administrator and by users who are employees to define the payment methods, view the invoices, and collect payments for these invoices. The second part of the module is *payments*, used by users (consumers) to view their invoices and pay them:

- *Payments management UI flow*: From the Payments management home page, the user can navigate to the Payment Methods page to search, view, add, modify, or delete payment methods. From this page, they can go to the Payment Method page, which works in view, edit, and add modes, to manage the data of the payment method. The home page also leads to the Invoices page. To view invoice details, the user then goes on to the Invoice page and can pay the invoice by navigating to the Pay page. To view the payments, the user can navigate from the home page to the Payments page. Users can search payments and view payment details on the Payment page.

- *Payments UI flow*: From the Payments home page, the user can view his invoices by navigating to the My Invoices page. Invoice details are available on the Invoice page. The user can pay the invoices by navigating to the Pay page and can view their payments by navigating from the home page to the My Payments page. They can search payments and view payment details on the Payment page.

Payment Methods Page

The Payment Methods page displays the methods and the *executers*. Every payment method has an executer to do the payment. For example, if the payment method is an online gateway, the executer is the class in the system that contains the code responsible for opening the payment gateway and confirms the payment is done successfully through it. In addition, the executer is responsible for saving the transaction's detail on the accounts. The user can add, edit, or delete a payment method. Figure 14-3 shows the Payment Methods page.

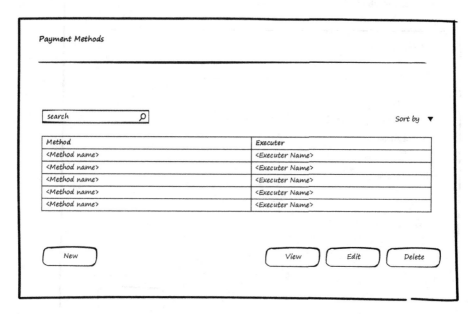

Figure 14-3. *Manage Payment Methods*

Payment Method Page

Figure 14-4 shows a wireframe for the Payment Method page in edit mode, which can be used for editing or adding a payment method. A payment method has a name, an icon (displayed on the button on the Invoice page), and executer. The executer should be a file that contains a class to handle the payment done by this method.

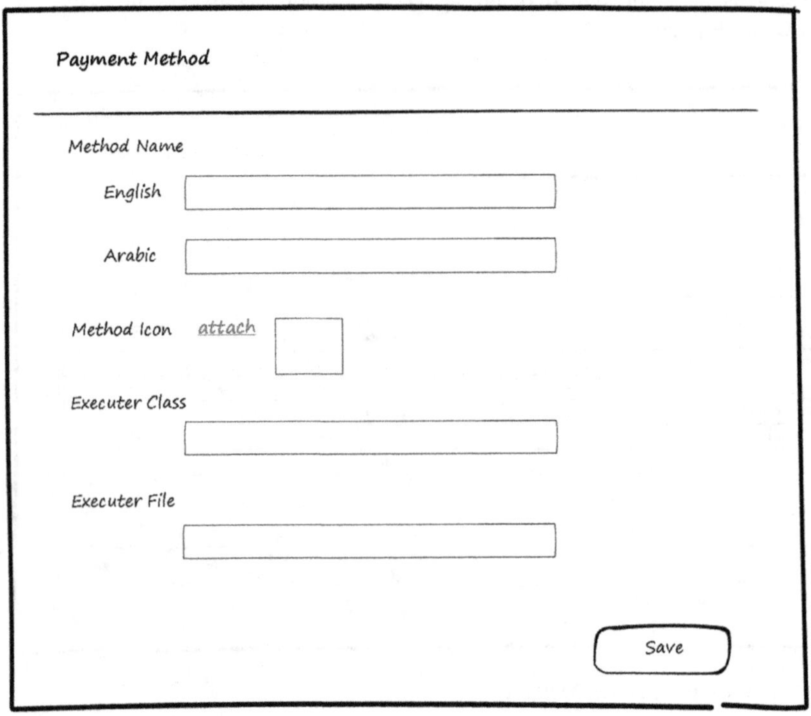

Figure 14-4. *Edit Payment Method*

The Payment Method page depends on the Localization module to support entering the payment method name in the supported languages.

Invoices Page

Figure 14-5 shows a wireframe for the Invoices page. From this page, the user can search invoices, view invoice details, or pay an invoice.

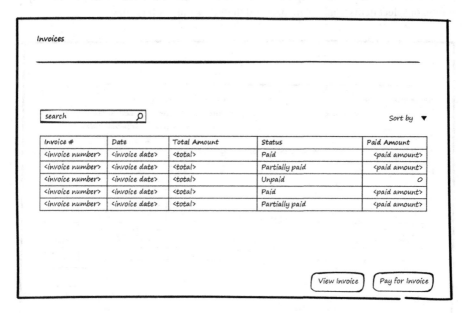

Figure 14-5. *List invoices*

Invoice Page

Figure 14-6 shows a wireframe for the Invoice page, which appears when the user selects an invoice from the Invoices page and chooses to view it. This page displays the details of the invoice and any payments applied to it. To pay the invoice, the user can click the Pay button or select items from the invoice and then click the Pay button.

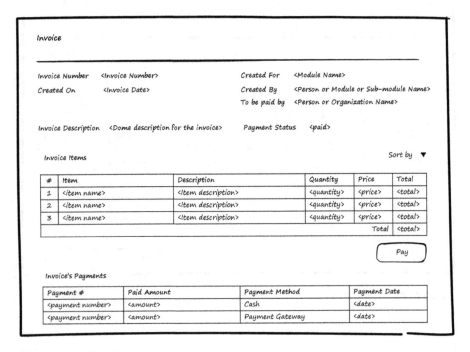

Figure 14-6. *View Invoice*

Pay Page

Figure 14-7 shows the Pay page that appears when user chooses to pay an invoice. It displays a summary of the invoice and allows the user to enter the amount of money they want to pay. The buttons at the bottom of the page represent the payment methods defined by the administrator. When the user clicks a button, the Payments module finds the associated executer class and starts it to perform the payment operation.

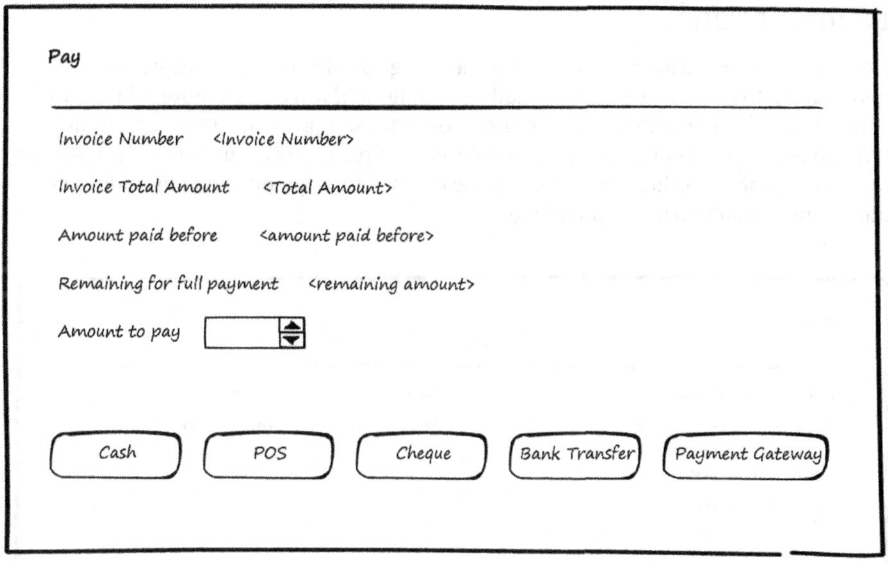

Figure 14-7. Pay

Payments Page

Figure 14-8 shows a wireframe for the Payments page. This page enables the user to search payments, view the payment details, or view the invoice associated with the payment.

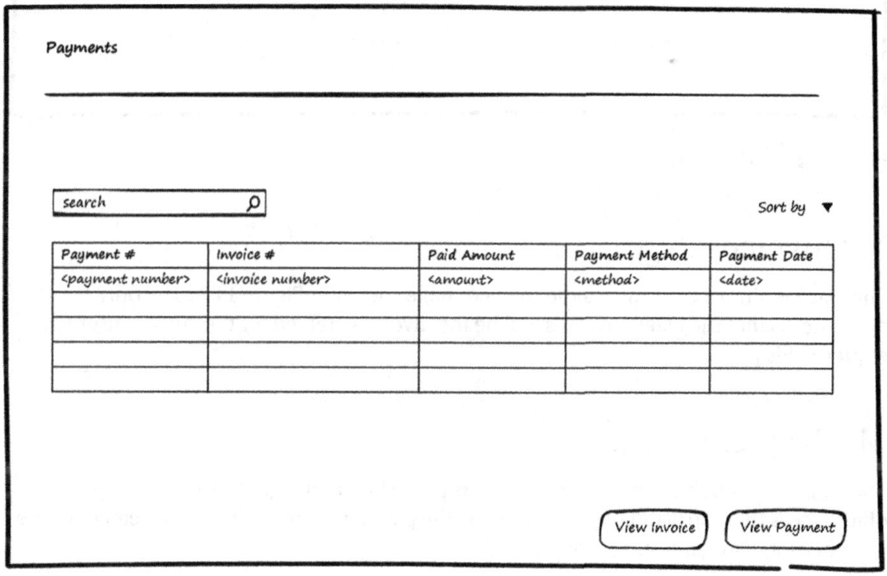

Figure 14-8. List Payments

Payment Page

Figure 14-9 shows a wireframe for the Payment page used to display the payment information. Note that the Payment Method Details field will display more information about the payment method and the transaction. For example, if the payment is done through online payment gateway, the details may be the gateway number, the transaction reference number, the last four digits of the card used for payment, and any additional information related to the payment method.

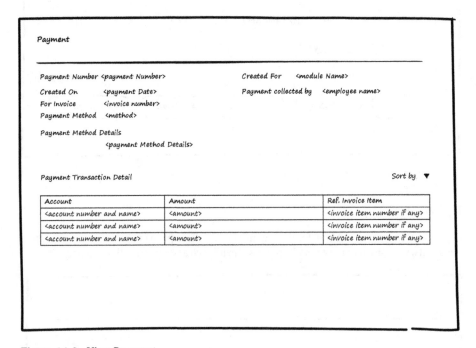

Figure 14-9. *View Payment*

My Invoices Page

This page is almost the same as the Invoices page shown in Figure 14-5. The only difference is that the listed invoices will be the invoices created for the current user who requests this page.

My Payments Page

This page is much the same as the Payments page shown in Figure 14-8. The only difference is that the listed payments will be the payments for the invoices created for the current user who requests this page.

Payments Module Entities

You've seen use-cases and wireframes for the Payments module, and now it's time to see the entities used by the Payments module to store the information needed to manage payments. Figure 14-10 shows the entities and the relations between them.

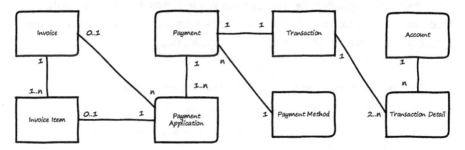

Figure 14-10. *Entities for the Payments module*

Here is a description for each entity:

- *Invoice*: Stores the invoice data generated by other modules.

- *Invoice Item*: Stores the items in the invoices (products or services). The modules that generate the invoice also generate these items.

- *Payment Method*: Stores data about the installed payment methods.

- *Payment*: Stores data about the payment for the invoice. For example, date of payment, paid amount, payment method, and so on.

- *Payment Application*: Payment can be done for the whole invoice or for just some invoice items. The Payment Application entity is used to store which invoice or which invoice's items the payment is made for.

- *Transaction*: Any payment will have a transaction that stores the money movement from source account to destination account(s). Every product (or service) in the invoice will be associated with an account to report its transactions. The Transaction entity stores the header information of the payment transaction.

- *Transaction Detail*: Stores the amounts of money moved from one account to another. It also stores the amounts for the source account and for the destination account(s).

- *Account*: This entity contains the accounts.

■ **Note** The executer class of the payment methods does the updates to the Transactions and Transaction Detail entities. The Payment module doesn't manage the Account entity—its responsibility is to allow other modules to generate invoices and allow users to pay for these invoices and track the payments. For the part related to accounts and transactions, the Payments module depends on the other modules to specify their destination accounts. In addition, the Payments module depends on the executer classes of the payment method to specify their source accounts and save the transaction details.

The relations between these entities can be summarized as follows:

- Invoice contains one or more invoice item.
- Payment is applicable on the whole invoice or on one or more invoice items.
- One Invoice can be paid by multiple payments.
- Payment is associated with one Transaction.
- Transaction should have at least two transaction details (one for the source account and the other for the destination account—it's possible to have multiple destination accounts).

Use of the Payments Module by Other Modules

Other modules give the Payments module their invoices that need to be paid, and those are managed by the Payments module. Giving invoice to the payment module can be done through the add invoice use-case and inquiring about the payment can be done through the get payment status use-case and the get payment info use-case.

Summary

This chapter discussed the Payments module, including use-cases and showing wireframes for the screens. I talked about the entities and their relations and about how other modules could use the Payments module.

CHAPTER 15

■ ■ ■

Signatures Module

In any organization, documents need to be signed and/or stamped by departments, employees, or people who deal with the organization. Nowadays *documents* usually mean *electronic documents*, which means every software system should support a mechanism to allow electronic and digital stamping and signing. The Signatures module's main functionality is to enable software systems to manage signatures by defining, performing, and validating them.

After finishing this chapter, you will be able to answer the following questions:

- What are digital and electronic signatures?

- What to be signed in the system and why?

- How should you store signature data?

- What does the UI for the Signatures module look like?

Signatures and Stamps

Signatures and stamps are used to verify the identity of the issuer of a document or approver of a document. There are two types of signature and stamps: digital and electronic.

- *Digital*: This involves hashing and encrypting data by the private key of the person who signs the data or an organization that stamps the data.

- *Electronic*: This involves appending an image to the data of the signature of a person who signed the data or the stamp of an organization that stamped the data.

Signatures and stamps can be used with documents provided to or provided by external entities. Using signatures and stamps with internal operations inside the organization is not recommended because it adds additional unnecessary effort (although some organizations ask to include signatures in their internal operations).

The Signatures module provides the functionality to manage signatures and stamps, allows users and organizations to digitally or electronically sign or stamp documents and data, and validates signed or stamped documents and data.

© Mohamed Farouk 2017
M. Farouk, *Infrastructure Software Modules for Enterprises*,
DOI 10.1007/978-1-4842-3021-3_15

Digital Signature and Electronic Signatures

Digital signature and electronic signature are used to ensure that a certain user signs data or a document. A *digital* signature encrypts documents or data with digital codes that are particularly difficult to duplicate. When data changes, it will no longer match the digital signature. An *electronic* signature means placing the user's signature image on a document. In order for an electronic signature to be used with data, we need to have a view template for the data, and the electronic signature will be appended to it.

Digital and Electronic Stamps

When documents or data are to be signed by an organization, the operation is called *stamping*. Every organization will have a stamp, which could be digital stamp, electronic stamp, or both.

A *digital* stamp encrypts documents or data with digital codes that are particularly difficult to duplicate. When data changes, it will no longer match the digital stamp. An *electronic* stamp places the organization's stamp image on a document. In order for electronic stamp to be used with data, we need to have a view template for the data, and the electronic stamp will be appended to it.

Every organization will have a list of authorized persons who can use the organization's stamp for stamping documents or data.

Singing or Stamping Documents and Data

The Signatures module manages signatures and stamps. In addition, it allows a person or organization to sign or stamp data and documents. It is the responsibility of the other modules to request signing or stamping for data and documents. The Signatures module provides the required user interface to perform the operation of singing or stamping and keeps a history of these operations that are requested and completed.

Signatures Module Use-Cases

Figure 15-1 shows use-cases for the Signatures module. Actors for these use-cases include any user for the system, an employee who represents an organization and can stamp for it, a user who has permission to manage the signatures and stamps, and the system modules that have data and documents to be signed or stamped by persons or organizations.

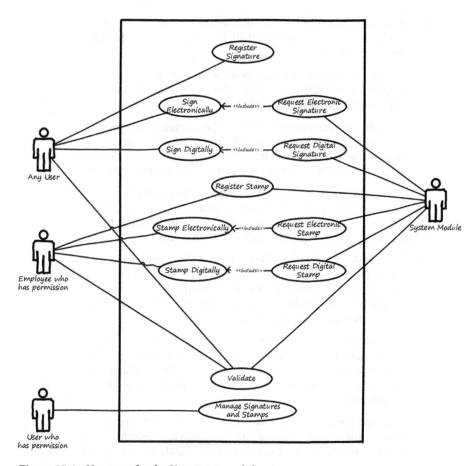

Figure 15-1. *Use-cases for the Signatures module*

Here is a description for each use-case:

- *Register signature*: This use-case enables any user to register or create a signature (electronic or digital) they can use to sign data and documents when needed.

- *Register stamp*: This use-case is used to enable authorized employees to register or create stamps (electronic or digital) for an organization to stamp data and documents when needed.

- *Sign Digitally*: This use-case enables the users, whose signatures are registered, to sign data and documents digitally.

- *Sign Electronically*: This use-case enables the users, whose signatures are registered, to sign data and documents electronically.

- *Stamp Digitally*: This use-case enables the authorized employees to stamp data and documents digitally using the registered stamp for the organization.

- *Stamp Electronically*: This use-case enables the authorized employees to stamp data and documents electronically using the registered stamp for the organization.

- *Request electronic signature*: This use-case enables modules to request signing data or documents electronically by a certain person. The use-case includes the sign electronically use-case to enable the specified person to provide their electronic signature.

- *Request digital signature*: This use-case enables modules to request signing data or documents digitally by a certain person. The use-case includes the sign digitally use-case to enable the specified person to provide their digital signature.

- *Request electronic stamp*: This use-case enables modules to request stamping of data or documents electronically by a certain organization. It includes the stamp electronically use-case to enable the authorized person in the organization to provide the electronic stamp of the organization.

- *Request digital stamp*: This use-case enables modules to request stamping of data or document digitally by a certain organization. It includes the stamp digitally use-case to enable the authorized person in the organization to provide the digital stamp of the organization.

- *Validate*: This use-case enables any user or module to provide documents or data with signatures or stamps and validates whether the document or data has a valid signature/stamp or not.

- *Manage signatures and stamps*: This use-case enables authorized users, based on their permissions, to manage the signatures and stamps (including adding, editing, deleting). Authorized users can also search signing and stamping operations that are completed.

Signatures Module Wireframes

This section shows high-level wireframe screens for the Signatures module. The UI flow is shown in Figure 15-2.

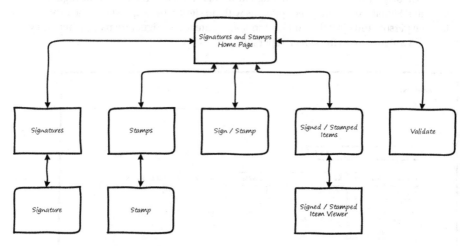

Figure 15-2. *UI flow for the Signatures module*

From the Signatures and Stamps home page, signatures can be managed by navigating to the Signatures page to search, view, add, or update signatures. From there the user can navigate to the Signature page, which works in different modes (view, edit, and add). To manage the stamps, the user goes to the Stamps page to search, view, add, or update stamps. From the Stamps page, the user can navigate to the Stamp page, which works in different modes (view, edit, and add).

The Sign/Stamp page is used to sign or stamp documents and data. It is accessible from the home page, or the user may be directed to this page when the other modules request signatures or stamps in the system.

By navigating from the home page to the Signed/Stamped Items page, the user can search and view the documents and data that were signed or stamped by users and organizations. To validate a signed or stamped item, the user navigates from the home page to the Validate page.

Signatures Page

Figure 15-3 shows a wireframe for the Signatures page. This page lists names of persons and allows the user to search them. If a person has a signature assigned to them, the system will display the date when this signature was created in the Electronic Signature and Digital Signature columns. For persons with no signature assigned yet, the user will select the person and click the Edit button to navigate to the Signature page, where they can assign a signature to the selected person.

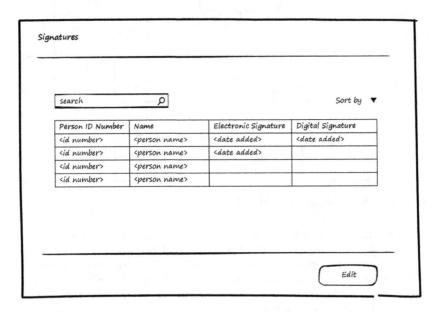

Figure 15-3. Manage Signatures

Signature Page

Figure 15-4 shows a wireframe for a person's Signature page, which displays the added signatures for the person. Signatures may change over time as the person may decide to change their signature. The system keeps a history of the signatures used by the user. On this page, the user can add a digital or electronic signature by clicking the corresponding button. The system will navigate the user to the page that creates the signature.

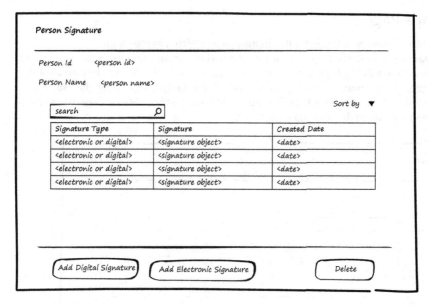

Figure 15-4. *Manage Person Signatures*

Figure 15-5 shows a wireframe for two pages. On the left is the page used for creating the electronic signature, and on the right is the page used for creating the digital signature.

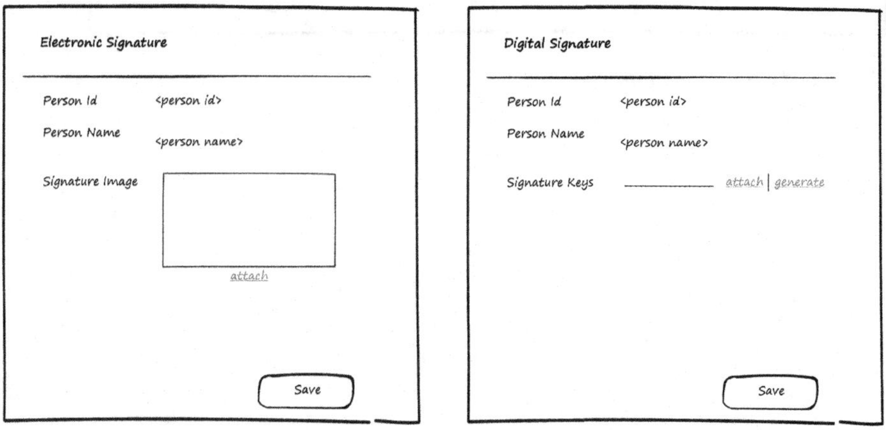

Electronic Signature

Person Id   <person id>

Person Name   <person name>

Signature Image

attach

Save

Digital Signature

Person Id   <person id>

Person Name   <person name>

Signature Keys   _____ attach | generate

Save

Figure 15-5. *Adding signatures*

Stamps Page

Figure 15-6 shows a wireframe for the Stamps page, which lists the names of organizations and allows the user to search them. If an organization has a stamp assigned to it, the system will display the date when the stamp was created in the Electronic Stamp and Digital Stamp columns. For organizations with no stamp assigned yet, the user will select an organization and click the Edit button to navigate to the Stamp Page, where they can assign a stamp to the selected organization.

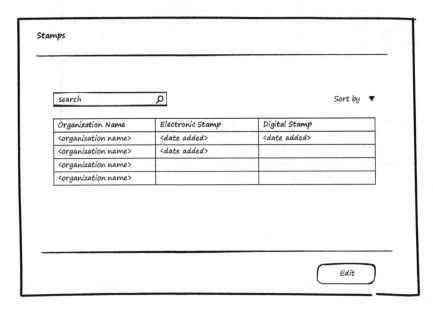

Figure 15-6. *Manage Stamps*

Stamp Page

Figure 15-7 shows a wireframe for an organization's Stamp page, which displays the added stamps for the organization. Stamps may change over time as the organization may decide to change its stamp. The system keeps a history of the stamps used by the organization. On this page the user can add a digital stamp or an electronic stamp by clicking the corresponding button. The system will navigate the user to the page that creates the stamp.

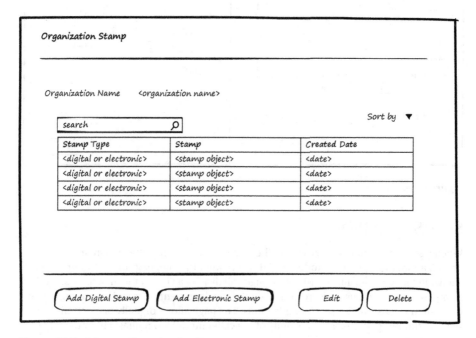

Figure 15-7. *Manage Organization Stamp*

Figure 15-8 shows a wireframe for two pages. On the left, you see the page used for creating the electronic stamp, and on the right is the page used for creating the digital stamp. It's necessary to add the authorized person(s) to use the stamp so that if the stamp is requested to be manually stamped, the system will display the stamp pages to the authorized user to perform the stamp operation.

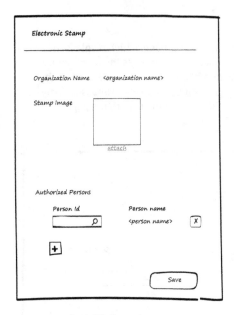
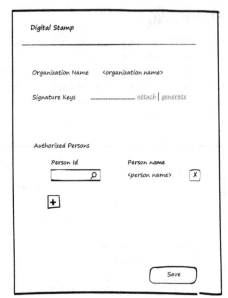

Figure 15-8. *Adding stamps*

Sign/Stamp Page

When a system module requests to get the signature or stamp of the person or organization, the Signature module will display either the Sign page or the Stamp page, shown in Figures 15-9 and 15-10. Every page will display a view of the data to be signed or stamped, and if persons who previously signed the document or organization stamped it, the system will list these users/organizations. The page allows digitally or electronically signing/stamping. It's the responsibility of the caller module to request either digital or electronic signature/stamp.

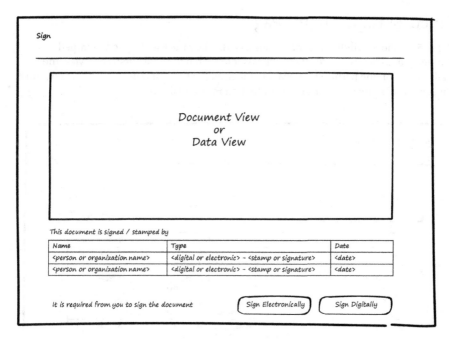

Figure 15-9. *Sign*

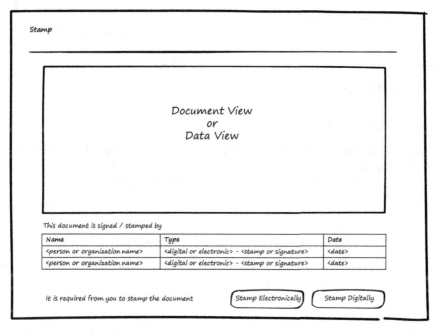

Figure 15-10. *Stamp*

205

Signed/Stamped Items Page

Figure 15-11 shows wireframe for the page that displays the list of signed/stamped documents or data. This page enables the user to search the listed items and view the details. Based on the permissions given to the user, they can view only items that contain their signature or organization stamp, or they can view all items.

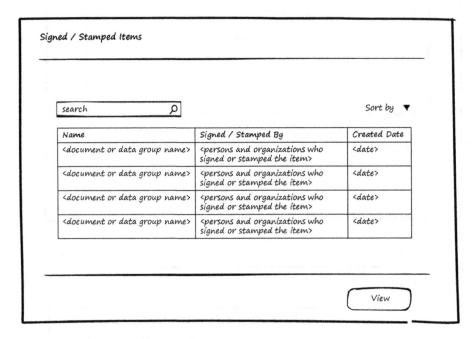

Figure 15-11. *List Signed/Stamped Items*

Singed/Stamped Item Page

In Figure 15-12, you see a wireframe for the page used to display the signed/stamped item details. The page displays the view of the document or data and lists the signatures or stamps done on the document, including by whom and when they were done.

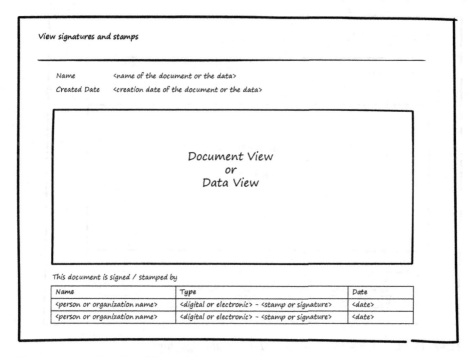

Figure 15-12. *View Signed/Stamped Item*

Validate Page

This page lets users attach a document file or data file to check whether the signatures or stamps inside these files are valid. Figures 15-13 and 15-14 show the cases for valid and invalid documents. For a valid document file or data file, the page will display list of recognized persons' signatures and organization stamps. For an invalid document file or data file, the page informs the user that this document or data is not valid.

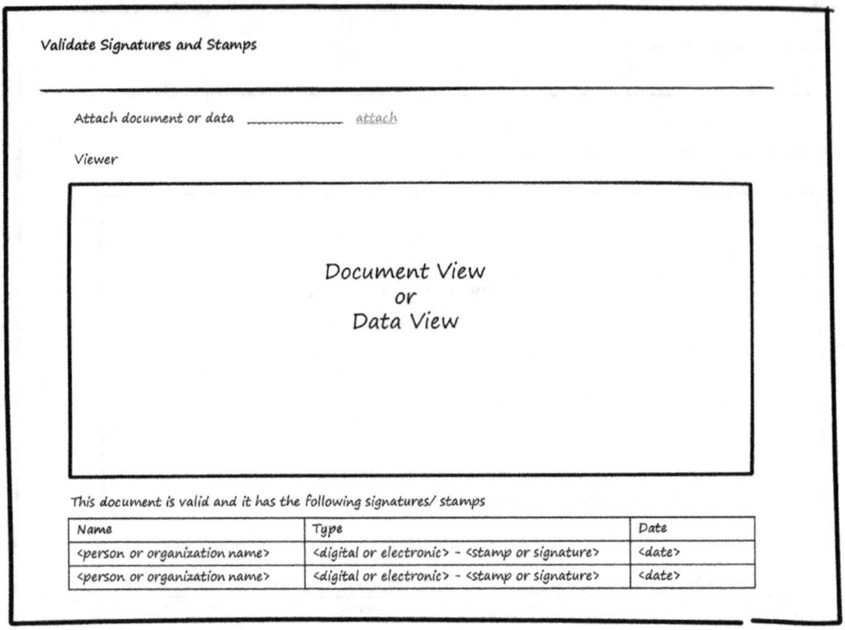

Validate Signatures and Stamps

Attach document or data _____ attach

Viewer

Document View
or
Data View

This document is valid and it has the following signatures/ stamps

Name	Type	Date
<person or organization name>	<digital or electronic> - <stamp or signature>	<date>
<person or organization name>	<digital or electronic> - <stamp or signature>	<date>

Figure 15-13. *Validate Signatures and Stamps: valid signature*

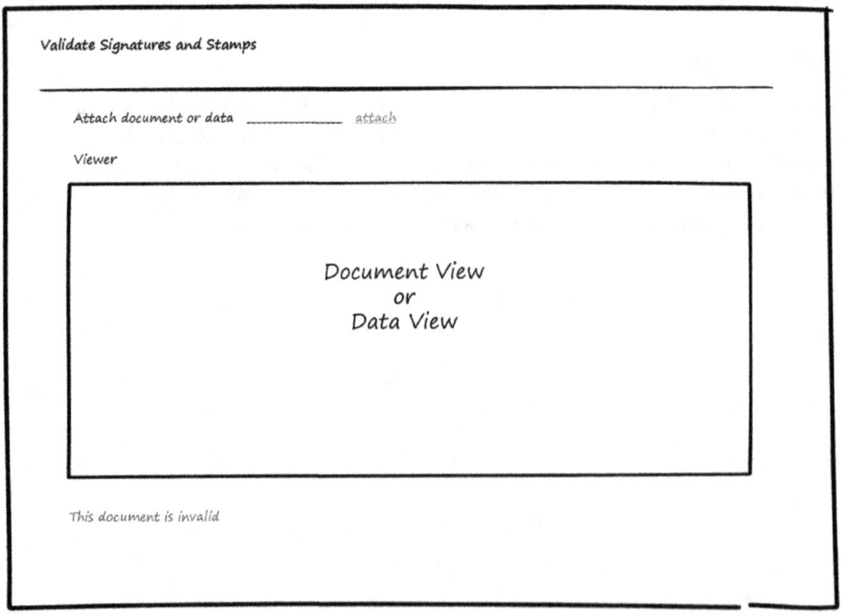

Validate Signatures and Stamps

Attach document or data _____ attach

Viewer

Document View
or
Data View

This document is invalid

Figure 15-14. *Validate Signatures and stamps: invalid signature*

Signatures Module Entities

You've seen the use-cases and wireframes for the Signatures module. Now it's time to see the entities used by the Signatures module to store the information needed to manage signatures. Figure 15-15 shows the entities and relations between them.

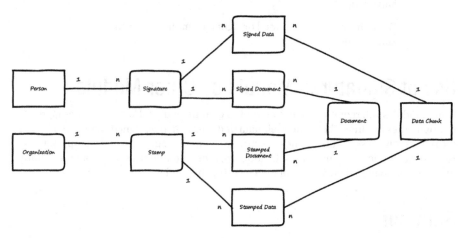

Figure 15-15. *Entities for the Signatures module*

Here is a description for each entity:

- *Signature*: Stores digital and electronic signatures for persons.

- *Stamp*: Stores digital and electronic stamps for organizations.

- *Document*: Stores documents to be signed (a document is a file that can be a in PDF or any Office file format).

- *Data Chunk*: Stores the chunk of data to be signed.

- *Signed Document*: Stores data about who signed the documents.

- *Signed Data*: Stores data about who signed the chunks of data.

- *Stamped Document*: Stores data about who stamps the documents.

- *Stamped Data*: Stores data about who stamps chunks of data.

The relations between these entities can be summarized as follows:

- Person can have multiple signatures.

- Organization can have multiple stamps.

- Documents can be stamped or signed by multiple signatures and stamps.

- Data Chunk can be stamped or signed by multiple signatures and stamps.

Use of Signatures Module by Other Modules

Other modules will request digital/electronic signature or digital/electronic stamp from the Signatures module. They send their data or document to be signed/stamped by using the request digital signature, request electronic signature, request digital stamp, and request electronic stamp use-cases. In addition, other modules can ask about the validity of the signed/stamped document or data by using the validate use-case.

Summary

This chapter discussed the Signatures module, including use-cases and wireframes for the screens. You saw the entities and their relations and found out how other modules could use the Signatures module.

CHAPTER 16

■ ■ ■

Conclusion

This book covered the software infrastructure modules, which are the base modules in any software systems. I discussed most of the functionalities supported by these modules, provided high-level wireframes for the UI, and discussed the entities to store the required data and relationships between them. Every module in the infrastructure modules provides essential services for other modules, whether they are system modules or business modules.

The infrastructure modules include the following:

- The Localization module manages the localizable resources.

- The Lookups module manages lookup data.

- The Documents module manages documents uploaded to the system.

- The Persons module manages persons' information.

- The Organization Structure module manages organizations and their relations, positions, and reporting hierarchies.

- The Authentication module manages authentication methods and authenticates users.

- The Authorization module manages services and permissions.

- The Communication Rules module manages and controls the way persons can communicate in the system.

- The Tasks module manages tasks assigned to persons.

- The Workflow module manages workflows' definitions and instances.

- The Notifications module manages notification methods and notifies persons.

- The Follow-Up module manages follow-up and reminds users about flagged items.

© Mohamed Farouk 2017
M. Farouk, *Infrastructure Software Modules for Enterprises*,
DOI 10.1007/978-1-4842-3021-3_16

- The Payments module manages payment methods and collecting payments for invoices.

- The Signatures module manages signatures and stamps and allows signing/stamping data and documents and validating signatures/stamps.

If a system contains the preceding modules as its base, other modules can better handle only their business and can depend on the infrastructure modules to provide the base services, as discussed through this book.

More About Infrastructure Modules

In this book, I discussed most of the infrastructure modules. Now I'll provide an overview of some topics I did not discuss.

More Functionality

For the modules covered in this book, there are two functions that I mentioned as currently out of scope for the book. I want to talk a little bit about them.

Authorization Module: Authorization to Access Data

As part of the Authorization module, there should be functionality to control data access by giving permissions on the data sets to be retrieved by users of the system. To do this, the Authorization module needs to have metadata for the data stored in the system. Metadata is a high-level layer giving information about the database tables and fields in a way that's understandable to system users. The Authorization module must be extended to include the use-case of managing data authorization. This is required by the system's administrators to build conditions on the data sets (to control the retrieved data) and assign these conditions to either Organization, Position Type, Position, Role, User, or Group (similar to giving permissions on functionalities, covered in Chapter 8).

Notifications Module: Notifications Among Software Systems or Modules

As part of the Notification module, there should be a functionality to send and receive notifications among systems or modules. This means the Notification module will need to be extended to include more use-cases to manage the notification methods that will be used by the modules or systems, manage the notification preferences for each module or system, and manage sending the notifications.

Additional Modules

Do you think I covered *all* the infrastructure modules? If so, please think again. There are indeed more infrastructure modules, and this section provides a brief overview of some of them.

Metadata Module

This module is responsible for managing the description of database tables and fields and giving them understandable names and descriptions. This module depends on the Localization module to ensure that these names and descriptions are localizable. The Metadata module alone doesn't provide a great value, but it does provide great value for other modules that depend on it: the Queries Builder Module, Reports Builder Module, and Business Rules Module. By having localizable names and descriptions for tables and fields, it's easier for users to build queries and reports, and it's easier for users or system administrators to manage the business rules.

Queries Builder Module

This module is responsible for enabling users to manage queries. *Queries* are sentences used to retrieve data from a database based on specific conditions provided by the user. Having this module in the system enables users to create queries and run them against the database. Users can also export the queries' results—thanks to the Metadata module for providing understandable names and descriptions for the database tables, which makes it easier for system users to use the Queries Builder module to create their own queries.

Reports Builder Module

This module is responsible for enabling users to manage reports. *Reports* are a visual representation of returned data from queries. Having this module in the system lets users design the layout of reports and associate queries with reports. The module is also responsible for generating reports based on the generation criteria defined by the users.

Business Rules Module

This module is responsible for managing business rules by enabling the system administrator to define or modify business rules. The module evaluates these rules when needed and can also display them to users when requested. *Business rules* are conditions to be checked by the system while users perform actions in the system or while the system is performing internal actions. An example of a business rule might be that an employee can't request vacation with a duration greater than their vacation balance. Business rules may be simple rules that are checked against static values, or they may be complex rules checked against dynamic values returned from the database. To handle these complex rules, the Business Rules module depends on the Queries Builder module.

Backup and Restore Module

This module is responsible for managing the backup and restore of the system's database and files. *Backup* means making a copy of the database and any files (documents) attached to the system. *Restore* means getting this database and files back to the system in case problems occurred in the system or data was destroyed—for example, in a disaster. Most systems depends on data center administrators to handle backup and restore by using the tools provided in the operating system and database management system. But having a module for backup and restore is better for the following reasons:

- It allows managing the backup and restore by the system's administrators, not the data center administrators.

- The module knows exactly what is databased and what files need to be saved. There is no dependency on humans to memorize.

- The Backup and Restore module depends on the functionality of the operating system and the database management system to perform its operations. This means there will be no missing feature of the backup and restore operations—just an easy interface to handle the backup and restore.

Figure 16-1 shows the dependency relationship among the modules discussed just now.

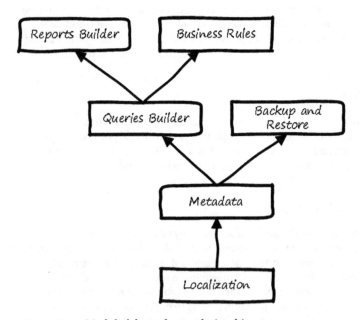

Figure 16-1. *Modules' dependency relationships*

The dependences are as follows:

- The Metadata module depends on the Localization module.

- The Queries Builder module and Backup and Restore Module depend on the Metadata module.

- The Reports Builder module and Business Rules module depend on the Queries Builder module.

Business Modules and Infrastructure Modules

As mentioned in Chapter 1, modules can be categorized as business modules and infrastructure modules. In this section, I provide two examples of simplified business modules and discuss how they can depend on the infrastructure modules.

Example 1: Vacations Module

The Vacations module is part of the Human Resources Management System. It goes under the category of Internal Services as it serves the employees inside the organization. The main functionality of the Vacations Module is, not surprisingly, to manage vacations. The module allows employees to request vacations and track their request status. The module also allows searching for approved vacations. Here is how the Vacations Module interacts with the infrastructure modules:

- It uses the Localization module to register the resource files and resource tables and retrieve the resources values based on the preferred language for the user of the system. The resource can then be managed from the Localization module.

- It uses the Lookups module to register the Vacation Types lookup.

- It uses the Documents module to register the document types and bundles that could be attached with the vacation requests. The documents definition can then be managed from the Documents module.

- It uses the Persons module to retrieve the employees' main information and contact information.

- It uses the Organization Structure module to get information about employees' positions and departments.

- It uses the Authorization module to register its services, which could be (for example) vacation request, extend vacation request, cancel vacation request, and search vacations. For users to use the Vacation module services, the permissions can be managed from the Authorization module.

- It uses the Workflows module to register the workflows definitions for the requests, and the workflows definitions can then be managed from the Workflows module. In addition, the Workflows module depends on the Tasks module to perform the workflow tasks and on the Notifications module to notify users about their request's status.

Example 2: Subscriptions Module

The Subscription module is part of the Club Management System. It goes under the category of Public Services because it serves the members of the club. These members are not employees of the club, so we can consider them as clients of the organization. The main functionality of the Subscription module is, of course, to manage subscriptions. The module allows members or candidate members to request subscriptions, renew subscriptions, or cancel subscriptions. Here is how the Subscription module interacts with the infrastructure modules:

- It uses the Localization module to register the resource files and resource tables and to retrieve the resources' values based on the preference language of the user of the system. The resources can then be managed from the Localization module.

- It uses the Lookups module to register the subscriptions types lookup.

- It uses the Documents module to register the document types and bundles that may be attached with the subscription requests. The documents' definitions can then be managed from the Documents module.

- It uses the Persons module to retrieve a member's main information and contact information.

- It uses the Authorization module to register its services. The permissions for users to use the Subscription module services can then be managed from the Authorization module.

- It uses the Workflows module to register the workflows definitions for the requests. The workflows definitions can then be managed from the Workflows module. In addition, the Workflows module depends on the Tasks module to perform the workflow tasks and on the Notifications module to notify users about their request's status.

- It uses the Payments module to add the subscription invoice that needs to be paid and to track the payment status of the invoice. The payment operation can then be managed from the Payments module.

- It uses the Signatures module to request digital or electronic signatures for generated club membership contracts. The signing operation for these contracts can then be managed from the Signatures module.

Implementing the Infrastructure Modules

If you are working on projects in which you build software systems from scratch, or if you have a small software product and want to move it to the next level, you need to consider including the infrastructure modules in your software system. This can take some time, but once finished they will be part of your system with the completely flexible functionalities they provide. You will then be able to re-use them in any project. You will have a system that has the main infrastructure functionalities of large enterprises.

You can start to develop these modules and use them in your existing software product or future projects. During development, you may find new ideas or more functionalities to add. You can then go back and enhance your infrastructure modules. Software development is an iterative process, and you gain more understating through time after completing an iteration. Figure 16-2 shows general iterations for implementing any software system or software module.

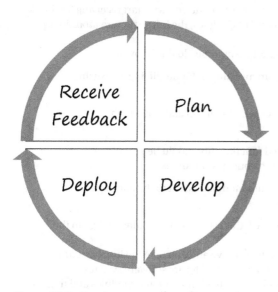

Figure 16-2. *Iterateve process for software systems or modules*

Plan

In this stage, you select the infrastructure modules you want to implement based on their dependency and your business modules needs. You may also include any new functionality you have collected from the previous iteration's feedback stage that you think may enhance your modules.

Develop

In this stage, you design the database and the architecture of the module, write the code, integrating the infrastructure modules with the business modules, and test the modules.

Deploy

In this stage, you deploy your software system to the production environment. Users and system administrators will be using it and will interact with your business modules and infrastructure modules. They will find out things are becoming more flexible and will take more control over system behaviors.

Receive Feedback

After having your system in a production environment, you will start receiving feedback about the system modules—for both types of modules, the infrastructure modules and the business modules.

For the requests related to infrastructure module, do the following:

- State the request for new functionality or for modifying an existing functionality.

- Study the request and check whether it will add value to the module.

- Ask whether this requested functionality should be part of the infrastructure modules or the business modules.

- If it is part of the infrastructure modules, add it to the backlog to plan for future iterations.

After processing the feedback, you will then start a new iteration and go to the planning stage once again.

Feedback from users will help you to improve and enhance the infrastructure modules. This in turn will enhance your current and future software systems.

I hope this book helped you to understand the infrastructure modules and that it will help you to move your software system to the next level.

Index

© Mohamed Farouk 2017
M. Farouk, *Infrastructure Software Modules for Enterprises*,
DOI 10.1007/978-1-4842-3021-3

Get the eBook for only $5!

Why limit yourself?

With most of our titles available in both PDF and ePUB format, you can access your content wherever and however you wish—on your PC, phone, tablet, or reader.

Since you've purchased this print book, we are happy to offer you the eBook for just $5.

To learn more, go to http://www.apress.com/companion or contact support@apress.com.

Apress®

Printed in the United States
By Bookmasters